D1031711

745.2 HAY
Hayek, Lisa,
Retro & vintage design

ILLINOIS PRAIRIE DPL

A65602 026574

RETRO&VINTAGE DESIGN

Lisa Hayek

RETRO&VINTAGE DESIGN

BRAUN

ILLINOIS PRAIRIE DISTRICT LIBRARY

CONTENTS

Preface

by Dagmar Glück

Retro is trendy and a fundamental design concept at the same time. Artists and architects have always looked to the past when creating something new. The Renaissance revived classical antiquity, Romanticism remembered medieval mysticism. What about us?

We celebrate revivals. Horn-rimmed glasses are back, leggings and jumpsuits, neon, checkered shirts, even cropped tops. We live a mix of pop and punk, nerd and rock singer Nena. What decade is this exactly? It is hard to tell as one retro wave chases the next. It is no longer about keeping pace with the latest trend. Instead, everyone is free to choose from the bits and pieces of past trends and subcultures whatever makes them happy and underscores their individuality. This goes far beyond the choice of clothing. Retro is omnipresent - Swing is back, so are Soul and Rockabilly. At the cinema there are sequels and prequels, at home we watch old TV series on DVD. Retro gaming is in, along with retro tattoos and retro bikes. At the same time, kidney-shaped coffee tables and lounge chairs are celebrating a comeback in our living rooms and at our favorite cafés, where we order apple cake that tastes (almost) the same as it did on Sunday afternoon in grandma's parlor.

As our world seems to revolve ever faster, the shapes, colors, scents, and tastes of our childhood serve as our anchors. We like to resort to familiar things when faced with today's excessive supply of disposable items and the pressure to constantly update. This is why we love retro and vintage products so much. "Retro & Vintage Design" is like a long-awaited meeting with good old friends. The following pages present 20th century objects that enjoyed a comeback in their old shape or as revised editions, but also many new products that are reminiscent of golden times but actually contain cutting-edge technology.

The term vintage was originally coined to describe valuable wines and cigars. When second-hand stores and flea markets shed their dingy image in the 1990s, vintage came to denote everything that is old and desirable. Vintage design aims to remain true to the original, but also sometimes uses innovative materials, improved manufacturing methods, and the latest technology. Notable examples include the 1960s mixer by KitchenAid, Gazelle bicycles, or the Desert Boots by Clarks, which all have a cult status today. Other brands live through constant innovations, but are also successful when reissuing their classics. For example, Puma and Adidas are reintroducing jerseys and shoes from the years 1954-74 for the Football World Cup 2014.

The borders between vintage and retro design are not clearly demarked. The British cult lamp Anglepoise of the 1930s is today available as an oversized floor lamp - true to the original but with a brand new size. Some classics have gone through various redesigns so that it is hard to tell where vintage ends and retro starts. In the 1960s, Yves Saint Laurent designed espadrilles with platform soles. Today the traditional workers' shoe is once again available, as a low heel version and in fresh colors, handmade by Ramoncinas in Spain.

We do not only have a nostalgic relationship to products from our own youth. Thanks to mass media we are also very familiar with trends and style icons of earlier generations. Therefore, creative professionals have a wealth of possibilities and can draw on the design history of the entire 20th century as a fund for new interpretations. For example, the Fiat 500 has received a futuristic facelift. The formerly cost-efficient first car of Italian families has become a stylish means of transportation for metropolitan singles. Retro design is often playful and humorous. Austin Yang proved to have a great sense of irony, when he brought the obsolete typewriter into the 21st century, turning it into the iTypewriter - the ultimate retro gadget for the iPad.

These and many more examples from "Retro & Vintage Design" showcase how innovative looking back can be. Retro is much more than reproducing past successes. The bandwidth of expression extends from newly interpreted cult objects via humorous references to ironic cultural critiques.

Fashion & Accessories

This is how retro styles used to emerge in earlier times: subcultures established a style that gradually evolved into a trend, finally reaching the mainstream, only to disappear when everyone grew tired of it. Then 15 to 20 years later the youth of the former era was once again ready for the return of the fashion. Until the 1990s, subcultures were clearly distinguishable by their styling - whether Punk, Mod, Hip-Hop or Indie. Today, there are no definite subdivisions anymore. New fashion trends are detected and marketed by trend scouts at such a speed that almost no trends can be clearly associated with a specific scene.

At the same time, the frequency of retro waves has increased rapidly or, as Karl Lagerfeld said: "Once fashion becomes out of fashion it is once again fashionable." For the ultimate street style, the urban bohemian can freely choose from the large wardrobe of the 20th century, from the roaring twenties to the nineties. Must-haves are brands and classics such as adidas and Converse, college jackets and trench coats. Some of these icons are presented in the following chapter. Such as the Wayfarer by Ray Ban. Introduced to the market in 1952, the model became a favorite of movie stars, was unfashionable for a long time, and today it is once again a universal fashion presence on every street.

In addition to the successful combination of different style and cult objects, unconventional unique items particularly highlight the individuality of the wearer. Vintage is the nonplus ultra trendy style. During the 1990s, trendsetters discovered second-hand fashion. With a bit of luck, one can discover at flea markets a very special item of clothing that is guaranteed not to be found in anyone else's closet. This search for the unique is further fuelled by eBay and online shops. Unfortunately, original well-preserved vintage brand clothing items are very rare and extremely sought after. New issues and vintage designs that resemble these "it" pieces are therefore a welcome alternative.

The charm of originals is based on the history they have participated in. However, the brands and redesigns of the following pages also tell their own unique stories. Designer Catherine Martin, for example, went through the Tiffany archives of records of the 1920s. This time travel to the Art Deco era inspired her to design breathtaking pieces of jewelry for Baz Luhrmann's remake of "The Great Gatsby". A truly one-of-a-kind unique product was the basis for Freemans Sporting Club's Dewars Toll Roll, a leather pannier that can double as a toiletry bag. Originally, Tommy Dewar used it to transport his father's whisky.

Davida Classic

For over thirty years this British brand has been manufacturing high-quality helmets and motorcycling accessories. Its designs and traditional colors are inspired by racers and street cultures of the past. One of the first helmets manufactured for motorcycle racing in the 1950s, the Davida Classic retains all the features of the original low dome racing helmet. The quilted neck curtain is made from soft leather and lined with brushed cotton, which provides additional security, while adding to its retro look. In addition, the numerous vintage designs of the shell replicate a former time's experience of motorcycling.

DESIGNERS: Davida UK Ltd. (UK)
MANUFACTURERS: Davida UK Ltd.
ORIGINAL: 1980s
RELAUNCH: 2012

PHOTOS: DAVIDA ARCHIVE

ADOPTED Leather Wrap Case for iPhone 5/5s

Reminiscent of the timeless, vintage rangefinder esthetic, the flowing lines of this Clemence-like leather case and the elegantly contrasting non-conductive metalized frame assure good haptic stimuli. With its slim-line silhouette, this case fits the iPhone 5 perfectly, at the same time protecting it reliably. There are eleven different colors and models available, ensuring that everyone's taste will be met with this classic design. The Leather Wrap Case pays homage to a classical optical device and provides an exciting contrast to the technology of the iPhone.

DESIGNERS: ADOPTED / David Watkins (USA)
LAUNCH: 2013

PHOTOS: ADOPTED

Adidas Europa TT, Retro World Cup Shirts, Stan Smith Sneaker

Inspired by 1970s designs, these sports jackets have a slim fit and familiar material along with the iconic three stripes on the arms and retro colors. In time for the World Cup, Adidas launched its series of retro jerseys. Each is inspired by vintage models from a country, the German one, for example, is modeled on the 1954 jersey, when Germany won the World Cup. Another heritage design, Adidas Originals reissued the iconic Stan Smith of the 1970s, made popular by the famous tennis player. With its clean lines and minimal design the remake stays true to the original. The white leather features the characteristic perforated stripes on the side and color accents on the back and tongue.

DESIGNERS: Adidas Originals (Germany)
ORIGINALS: 1970s
RELAUNCH: 2014
LAUNCH WORLD CUP SHIRTS: 2014

CREDIT: THE STAN SMITH WORD MARK, TREFOIL LOGO AND THE 3-STRIPES LOGO ARE
TRADE MARKS OF THE ADIDAS GROUP USED WITH PERMISSION

Hudson Made:
Beard and Shave Soap

Hudson Made is an online boutique selling handmade products from the Hudson Valley, New York. The Beard and Shave Soaps generate a lather that acts as both a gentle beard shampoo and an exceptional shaving cream. The three distinct aromas as well as the soaps' packaging conjure a 19th-century feel, when each item was still individually boxed and packed by hand. The small production batches along with the exact location of production gives the brand a sense of authenticity in an increasingly global marketplace.

DESIGNERS: Hovard Design (USA)
DISTRIBUTORS: Hudson Made

PHOTOS: HUDSON MADE, NY

Ray-Ban Wayfarer and Aviator Full Color

In 1929 Ray-Ban created a new type of eyewear that protected pilots from glare at high altitudes. The first model available to the public was a plastic frame in the Aviator shape which went on sale in 1937 making the eyewear a popular fashion accessory. In 1952 the best-selling Wayfarer was launched, soon becoming the favorite accessory of movie stars. This season, Ray-Ban launches its icons in new styles. For the first time ever, the Wayfarer is dressed in leather, wrapped around the frame like a glove. The Aviator also gets a fresh new look in pastel colors. This gives the classic gold frame a new look yet keeps it very retro with gold, red or blue lenses reminiscent of 1970s gangsters.

DESIGNERS: Ray-Ban (Italy)
MANUFACTURERS/DISTRIBUTORS: Luxottica Group S.p.A.
ORIGINALS: 1937 (Aviator), 1952 (Wayfarer)
REDESIGN: 2014

PHOTOS: LUXOTTICA S.P.A.

Reebok Freestyle Hi Vintage, Pump Vintage Pack

With the release of these two vintage sneakers, Reebok brought back the icons of the 1980s and 1990s. Originally designed for aerobics, the Freestyle Hi quickly became one of the most popular athletic shoes of all time. After countless remakes, it became a bit quiet around the shoe at the turn of the millennium. With this Freestyle release, however, Reebok celebrates those good old days, relaunching the shoe in proper vintage red and blue suede with contrast laces. An icon of the 1990s basketball scene, the Pump was the first shoe featuring an internal inflation mechanism to provide stability around the ankle. For 2014, Reebok revives the Pump in four neat vintage looks.

DESIGNERS: Reebok (Germany)
ORIGINALS: 1984 (Freestyle Hi), 1989 (Pump)
RELAUNCH: 2013 (Freestyle Hi), 2014 (Pump)

PHOTOS: REEBOK, 43EINHALB SNEAKER STORE. 43EINHALB.COM (P. 21)

The Great Gatsby Collec-tion by Tiffany & Co.

The Great Gatsby Collection was designed for Baz Luhrmann's film in collaboration with designer Catherine Martin. The spectacular jewelry is based on 1920s designs from the Tiffany archives. The collection underlines the style, glamour and lavishness of the time, featuring an Art Deco-inspired ring of tanzanite stones, diamonds and platinum, a hand ornament with a daisy motif in diamonds and cultured pearls, a bracelet of diamonds and seed pearls with a Chinoiserie-inspired pattern, and a pearl necklace with tassel pendants of diamonds and pearls. The collection also includes a women's card case of sterling silver and white enamel, and a slim flask of sterling silver and black enamel for the men.

DESIGNERS: Tiffany & Co. (USA)
COLLABORATING DESIGNER: Catherine Martin
LAUNCH: 2013

PHOTOS: TIFFANY & CO.

BALLY – Curling, Scribe, Stripe

The Swiss brand recently reintroduced some icons, including the Curling, the Scribe and the Stripe. The unique shape of the Curling with its water-resistant sole and pointed toecap has remained, while a high shaft in lambskin was added, giving it a contemporary look. Bally consistently reinvents its iconic men's shoe, the Scribe, while keeping its traditional craftsmanship and comfort. This model combines an alligator upper with a casual loafer style. The Stripe collection features the re-engineered, iconic red and white stripe inspired by Swiss trains passing by at high speed. The new stripe is made of soft calf leather adding a touch of understated luxury to the chestnut-colored vintage bags.

DESIGNERS: BALLY (Switzerland)
MANUFACTURERS/DISTRIBUTORS: BALLY
ORIGINALS: 1951 (Scribe), 1956 (Curling)
REINTRODUCTION: 2012 (Scribe/Curling)
LAUNCH STRIPE: 2013

PHOTOS: BALLY SWITZERLAND

Borsalino Beaver

Once a men's classic, the Borsalino fedora enjoyed a comeback recently. In 1857 Giuseppe Borsalino created the distinctive design of the hat in Italy. Inspired by the crushed bowler hats of the men in the Risorgimento, Borsalino designed the iconic middle crease or "vaga" for his hat. To easily lift the hat in presence of a lady, he added two slight dents at the front of the crease, the "bozze" or pinches. Each hat is handmade using fur felt in a process that takes an average of seven weeks. Due to its elegance and practicality, this model became an icon, which is reinterpreted in different ways today. Whether in light colors or dark, with a wide or slim brim, each hat is a unique piece of craftsmanship.

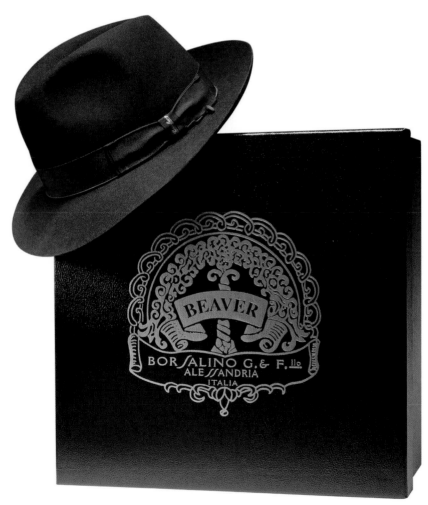

DESIGNERS: Borsalino's Style-Product Department (Italy)
ORIGINAL: 1857
REDESIGN: 1940s
RELAUNCH: 2002

PHOTOS: BORSALINO

Espadrilles

This shoe incorporates history and tradition with fashion and trendiness. It is said that the sandal was already worn in the 13th century by the infantry of King Aragon. The shoe of mineworkers in the 19th century, it entered the world of fashion in the 1960s when Yves Saint-Laurent commissioned an espadrille with a heel. This was a new take on the casual worker's shoe. Since then it has been reinterpreted in countless variations and was taken up by various fashion companies who produce the shoes all over the world. These particular pairs, however, are still entirely handcrafted in the region of La Rioja in Spain, both the braided rope sole and the upper cotton canvas are completely authentic.

DESIGNERS: Ramoncinas (Spain)
MANUFACTURERS: Ramoncinas
DISTRIBUTORS: Espadrillestore
LAUNCH: 2008

ILLINOIS PRAIRIE DISTRICT LIBRARY

PHOTOS: ALEXIS LANCIEN / ESPADRILLESTORE

**Design:
Ramoncinas**

ILLINOIS PRAIRIE DISTRICT LIBRARY

Casio Retro Collection A158WEA, A159WGEA

Founded in Tokyo, Casio's innovation and imagination has kept it going strong since 1957. In the 1980s the company created an icon with its golden digital watch, which evolved into the "must-have" of an entire generation due to Marty McFly in "Back to the Future". In 2011 Casio Europe relaunched its icon in fresh new variations. While the original octagonal design and digital face remain, the collection was extended by a model with a silver stainless steel wristband and new retro-looking faces for gold and silver wristbands. This collection makes you spoilt for choice, as every model constitutes the perfect accessory for any retro-lover.

DESIGNERS: Casio Europe GmbH (Germany)
ORIGINAL: 1980s
RELAUNCH: 2011

PHOTOS: CASIO EUROPE GMBH

The Chief Flight Suitcase

An American classic, the Chief Trunk Company is a revival of the Oshkosh Trunk Company once known as the United States' answer to Louis Vuitton. Upholding Oshkosh Trunk's standards of quality and craftsmanship, Chief Trunk produces travel/city bags and accessories with its hallmark red and yellow striped canvas: distinctive yet timeless,

fashionable yet practical, rugged yet refined. Inspired by the "American Good Life" the newly incarnated Chief Trunk creates collections for the modern lifestyle: travels, holidays, weekends, outings, gatherings and celebrations.

PHOTOS: MICHAEL SAMBRANO, NEW YORK

DESIGNERS: The Chief Trunk Company (USA)
LAUNCH: 2013

Clarks Originals Desert Boot

In 1949 Nathan Clark developed the indestructible Desert Boot. Its inspiration was a crepe-soled boot made from rough suede in Cairo's fabled Old Bazaar and the footwear of choice for off-duty Eighth Army officers during World War 2. Convinced that the shoe was equally suited as a leisure boot as it was for the army, he presented it at the Chicago Shoe Fair and returned to England with countless orders.

Revisiting timeless silhouettes, the traditional British footwear brand brings back its iconic Desert Boot, returning each season looking as fresh and stylish as ever, featuring a lace-up front and the brand's signature crepe sole. The rugged, yet elegant design of the ankle-high boot is the epitome of understatement and confident styling.

DESIGNERS: Clarks/Nathan Clark (UK)
ORIGINAL: 1949
REDESIGN: 2005

Design: Nathan Clark

PHOTOS: CLARKS

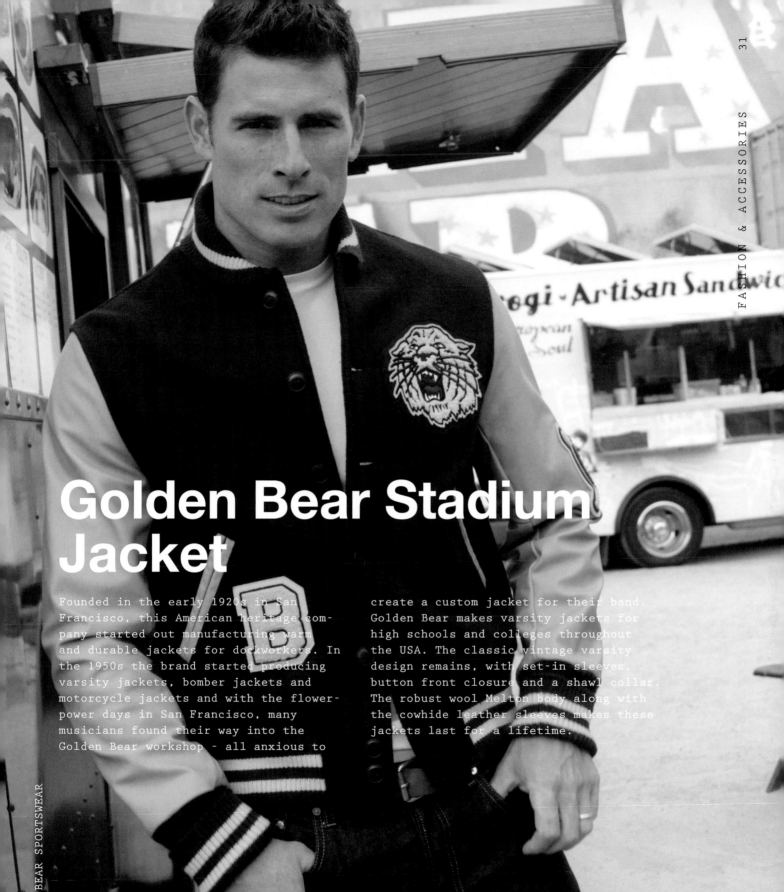

PHOTOS: GOLDEN BEAR SPORTSWEAR

Golden Bear Stadium Jacket

Founded in the early 1920s in San Francisco, this American heritage company started out manufacturing warm and durable jackets for dockworkers. In the 1950s the brand started producing varsity jackets, bomber jackets and motorcycle jackets and with the flower-power days in San Francisco, many musicians found their way into the Golden Bear workshop - all anxious to create a custom jacket for their band. Golden Bear makes varsity jackets for high schools and colleges throughout the USA. The classic vintage varsity design remains, with set-in sleeves, button front closure and a shawl collar. The robust wool Melton body along with the cowhide leather sleeves makes these jackets last for a lifetime.

DESIGNERS: Golden Bear Sportswear (USA)
MANUFACTURERS/DISTRIBUTORS: Golden Bear Sportswear
LAUNCH: 2013

Travel Roll

DESIGNERS: Freemans Sporting Club (USA)
LAUNCH: 2012

Designed as a special collaboration between NYC's influential menswear maker Freemans Sporting Club and Dewar's whisky, the limited-edition Travel Roll is what the brand is calling a "modern take on the vintage utility roll used by Tommy Dewar to carry his father's whisky around the world." The heavy-duty, 18 oz. waxed canvas bag features straps made from hand-cut English bridle leather and an overall look defined by FSC's subdued styling. While the suggested use is to sling a bottle of golden brown by bicycle, the Travel Roll can also be used as a large dopp kit.

PHOTOS: FREEMANS SPORTING CLUB

Dunlop Classic Crack Dispatch and Holdall

This British heritage brand is particularly popular in the world of tennis. Yet these vintage looking bags are great accessories for any occasion. The Classic Crack collection features a smaller dispatch bag and a larger hold-all. The models are vintage-inspired in classic black, navy or brown, all featuring a distressed leather look, emphasizing the vintage used appearance. Of course, the Dunlop metal logo can't be missed as well. While these bags will see to a retro appearance in the gym, they are also practical for everyday use out and about.

DESIGNERS: Dunlop Sport (UK)
DISTRIBUTORS: Wiley Accessories Ltd.
LAUNCH: 2002

PHOTOS: WILEY ACCESSORIES LTD

MMT Calendar

MMT Watches has reinterpreted the traditional pocket watch lending it contemporary elegance and the poetry of past timepieces. The unique haptic qualities of wood provide a soft yet firm feel in the palm of the hand. The successor of MMT Memento is available in two versions: walnut and rose gold or maple and silver. The Japanese three-hand movement with a date along with the genuine leather strap make this model an understated casual accessory ready to match any style from a 3-piece suit to a raw denim pair of jeans.

DESIGNERS: MMT Watches (Hong Kong)
FOUNDERS: Thomas Letourneux, Jeremy Guedez, Baptiste Guedez
LAUNCH: 2013

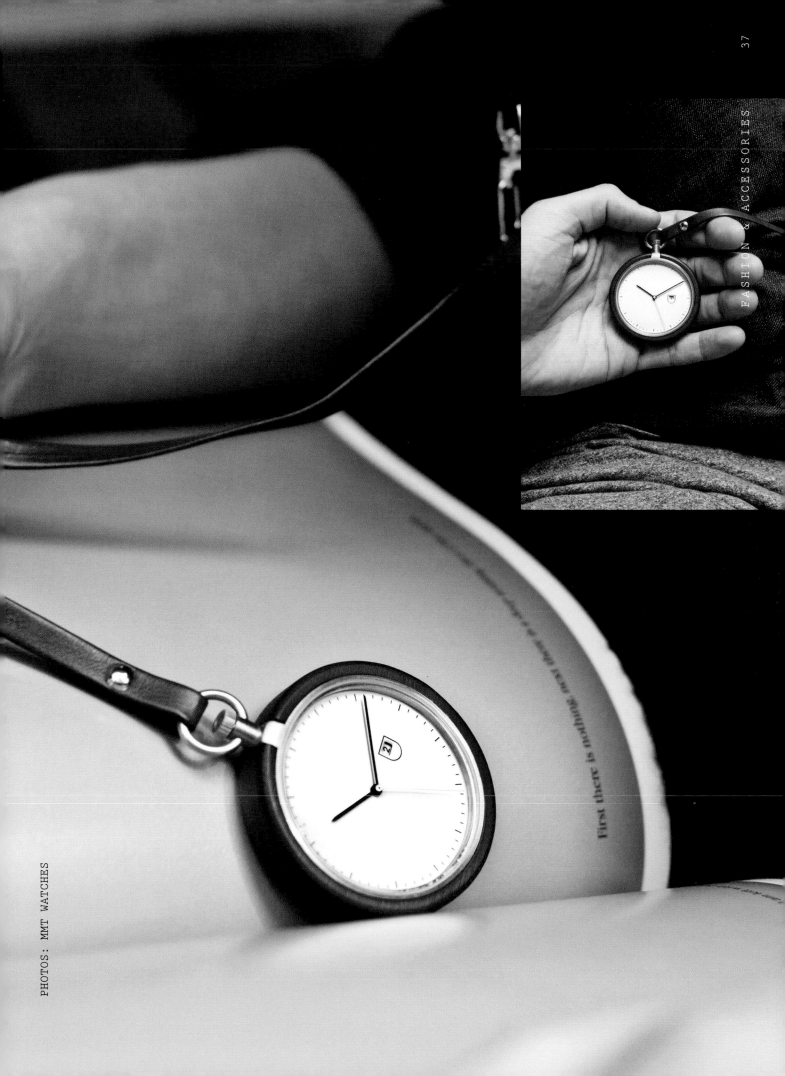

First there is nothing

PHOTOS: MMT WATCHES

SUPER Sunglasses

In 2007 Daniel Beckerman founded SUPER in Italy to design sunglasses "that all my friends would love to wear". A few years later, SUPER is a leading brand in high-quality yet affordable contemporary eyewear. The colorful acetate sunglasses are handmade in Italy, with extra quality added by the collaboration with the German lens company Zeiss, giving each piece excellent eye-protecting lenses.

Each of the featured models interprets a classic with a contemporary twist. Be it an "ode to Deco esthetics" (Panamá Edgar), a celebration of the classic explorer sunglasses (49er Classic Havana), or an homage to eccentric British tapestries (Paloma Pappagallo), these shades definitely have a retro vibe.

DESIGNERS: SUPER by Retrosuperfuture (Italy)
MANUFACTURER LENSES: Carl Zeiss
LAUNCH: 2012/2013

PHOTOS: SUPER BY RETROSUPERFUTURE

Rookie Retro and NuWave

Rookie has been making high-quality roller skates since 1978. Now in its third decade, Rookie Skate Company prides itself on making unique and stylish skates that no other company can match. The Rookie Retro keeps the 90s fresh; inspired by the classic high-top sneakers and in bright retro colors these skates will make you want to hit the streets right away. While the NuWave looks more contemporary, its color design is definitely retro. It comes with two pairs of laces in green or purple.

DESIGNERS: Rookie Skate Company (UK)
MANUFACTURERS: Rookie Skate Company
DISTRIBUTORS: Shiner Ltd.
ORIGINALS: 1978
RELAUNCH: 2014

PHOTOS: ROOKIE SKATE COMPANY

PICTO Watches

Rosendahl relaunched this iconic watch to mix up the current trends in men's and women's watches. Picto was first conceived in 1984 by Danish designers Christensen and Andersen who wanted to design a "picture" of time. As opposed to conventional watches where the hands show time on the face of the watch, the face of the watch rotates with a dot representing the hour. The sleek and minimalist esthetic coupled with bold colors and refined materials makes this watch very contemporary. The revised version features a supple silicone strap that can easily be detached from the face of the watch - introducing endless combinatory possibilities. The three different sizes and color combinations make this retro icon an ideal accessory for women and men.

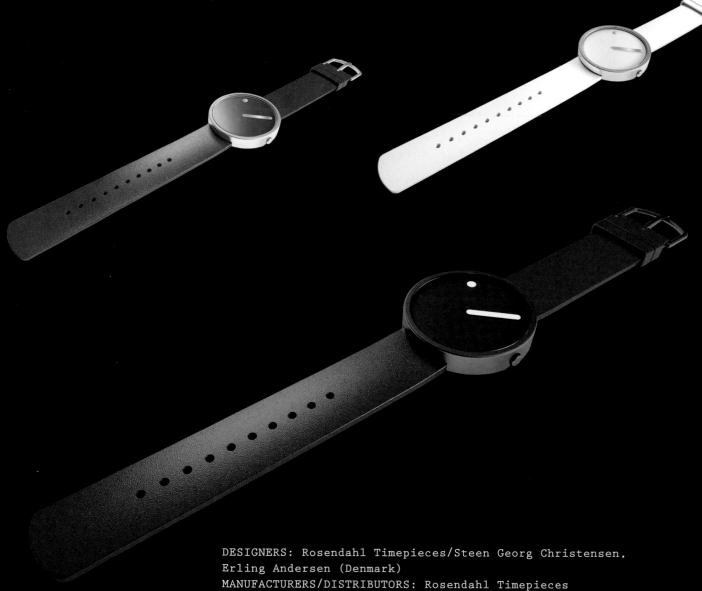

DESIGNERS: Rosendahl Timepieces/Steen Georg Christensen, Erling Andersen (Denmark)
MANUFACTURERS/DISTRIBUTORS: Rosendahl Timepieces
ORIGINAL: 1984
RELAUNCH: 2012

PHOTOS: ROSENDAHL TIMEPIECES

Puma Roma 68 Vintage

A sharp relic of the 1960s is back in the 21st century - the Puma Roma 68 Vintage trainers. Introduced back in 1968, the Puma Roma 68 was designed to honor the Italian National Football Team winning the European Cup in 1968. This re-worked vintage version is brought back in a plethora of colors, ranging from the classic black and white leather upper to a blue and yellow, and has a suede toe piece, a rubber mudguard, and the embroidered Puma logo on the tongue finished off with a rubber herringbone design sole.

DESIGNERS: Puma (Germany)
ORIGINAL: 1968
RELAUNCH: 2010

PHOTOS: PUMA

Footwear by Hard Graft

Previously known for their outstanding range of bags and first-rate wallets and accessories, Hard Graft's repertoire has been expanded to include some of the finest footwear. The London-based brand took its inspiration from historic boxing boots and other classics adjusting the design to contemporary esthetics. Each pair is made from the finest Italian leather, which has been vegetable tanned and colored with natural coloring made from tree bark to give it that premium color. Lined in soft calf leather with a leather, wood and rubber sole, these boots also include the wool and red/white ribbon detailing, which is the signature of Hard Graft's goods.

DESIGNERS: Hard Graft (UK)
LAUNCH: 2012

PHOTOS: HARD GRAFT

JanSport Heritage Series

JanSport was founded in 1967 in Seattle by three friends who had the original idea of building a better backpack for the outdoors. They set up business above a transmission shop, started making aluminum-frame packs, worked hard, had fun and never looked back. In 2009, the Heritage Series was launched as a way to share cherished styles from the past and reconnect today's youth culture with the rich history of JanSport. The series of packs features original details including Cordura® and nylon fabrics, seat belt webbing, brass zippers and hardware, and the brand's original woven label from 1967.

DESIGNERS: JanSport Design Team (USA)
MANUFACTURERS: JanSport
ORIGINALS: 1960s-1980s
RELAUNCH: 2009

PHOTOS: JANSPORT

Kaweco Liliput

In 1910 the German brand Kaweco first produced a Liliput fountain pen of ebonite. The remake of this series is now made of solid aluminum and comes in the colors black, silver and brass. For those who really like that vintage feel it is available as a fountain pen with steel nib - for the others, Kaweco also made a ballpoint version of the tiny pen. Only 97mm long when closed, the Liliput is one of the smallest fountain pens for standard ink cartridges in the world. The sleek cylindrical design and the light weight of eight grams due to the aluminum makes this the perfect travel companion, and will guarantee for a James Bond-like moment when taken out of the inside pocket of your suit.

DESIGNERS: Kaweco (Germany)
MANUFACTURERS: h & m gutberlet gmbh
ORIGINAL: 1910
REMAKE: 2012

PHOTOS: H & M GUTBERLET GMBH

Men's 1970s Levi's Jeans T-Shirt

Levi's Vintage Clothing revives designs from the Levi's archives dating back to 1873. The fabrics are authentically woven and dyed in an aspiration to get as close to the original as possible. This particular t-shirt is inspired by a 1970s archived design, featuring a retro-style print across the front. It has a relaxed fit and is crafted in the USA from thick premium cotton with a textured finish. The contrasting trims on the neck and sleeves' edges as well as the orange-colored banded tab on the lower side make this piece reminiscent of a time when flare pants and jeans jackets were en vogue.

DESIGNERS: Levi's Vintage Clothing (USA)
DISTRIBUTORS: oki-ni
ORIGINAL: 1970s
RELAUNCH: 2013

Tootal Scarves

Established in England in 1799, Tootal is one of the oldest surviving clothing brands. Like many British companies of the time, Tootal helped the war effort by manufacturing clothing for the armed forces. The Tootal Scarf itself became a popular fashion accessory in the World War 2 era, often associated with an "RAF" style and look. In the 1960s the Mod culture took up the retro scarves and

turned them into a style icon. In 2013 Tootal Vintage revived the retro paisley and polka dot designs in finest silk, making the scarves the perfect retro accessory for a dapper dandy look. In addition, the 2-ply style of the scarves not only makes them look great, but will also keep you warm on a windy day.

DESIGNERS: Stuarts London (UK)
MANUFACTURERS: Tootal Vintage
ORIGINAL: 1799
RELAUNCH: 2013

AN AUTHENTIC
TOOTAL
SCARF
REGD IN ENGLAND 1799

Camera Accessories by Hard Graft

With this new line of camera accessories by British designers Hard Graft, taking out your camera will be like opening a present every time. The premium vegetable-tanned Italian leather gets its heritage look from a traditional coloring technique that uses tree bark. This extremely soft leather also lives and will look more beautiful and individual the longer you have it. The camera bag is nice and compact for everyday use and protects your camera with a woolen felt-padded interior. The short camera handle lies comfortably in your hand and is flexible to use during the times you might not need a full shoulder strap. Combine the two and you're ready to take the perfect shot wherever you go. The designer's innovative iPhone cases are also not to be missed.

DESIGNERS: Hard Graft (UK)
LAUNCH: 2013

PHOTOS: HARD GRAFT

Porsche Design P'8478, P'8479

The secret lies in their simplicity: these iconic Porsche Design sunglasses combine signature sleek, lightweight design with functionality. The Exclusive Sunglasses became legendary through their special mechanism, which allowed changing the lenses. Back then, as well as now, these aviators are the chosen sunglasses of stars and celebrities. The Sports Sunglasses also hold a long standing celebrity tradition – the most prominent being Yoko Ono, which helped those futuristic looking shades to fame when she wore them to a press conference in the 1980s. With the current reproductions, Porsche Design pays homage to its iconic models from the 1970s, combining the original designs with high-quality materials.

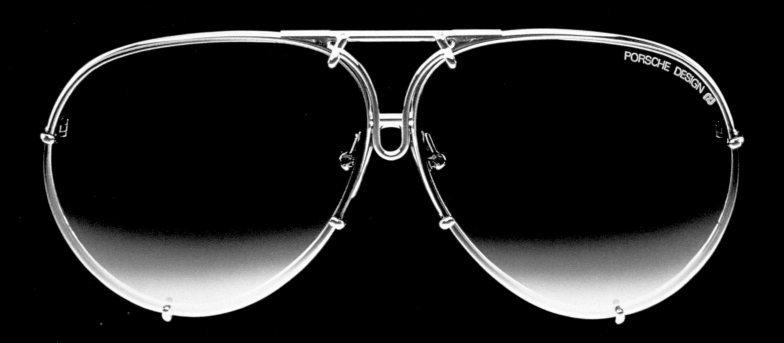

DESIGNERS: Porsche Design Studio (Austria)
MANUFACTURERS: Rodenstock
DISTRIBUTORS: Porsche Design
ORIGINALS: 1978 (Exclusive Sunglasses),
1979 (Sports Sunglasses)
RELAUNCH: 2008 (Exclusive Sunglasses as P'8478),
2009 (Sports Sunglasses as P'8479)

PHOTOS: PORSCHE DESIGN, GERMANY

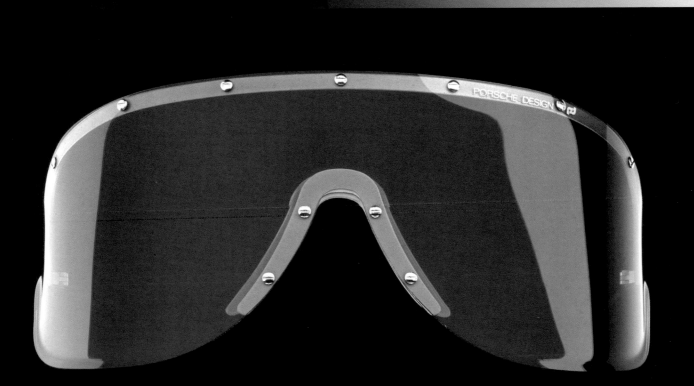

Home & Decor

The half-life of interior design trends is significantly longer than that of fashion. Anyone who has just disposed of old furniture is not likely to long for the 1990s. The esthetic of the "Mad Men" TV series is currently en vogue – the shapes of the 1950s and 1960s feature compellingly straight lines, dynamic curves, and slim shapes. In addition to timber and glass, high-quality plastics are primarily used, with white and soft pastel predominating, while graphic patterns and strong colors create accents.

The look is permeated by lightness and openness. While at the end of the 20th century one's own four walls were re-garded as an intimate retreat that should be rendered as cozy as possible, today's private spaces have become much more public. Homing has replaced cocooning. Friends are invited over for game nights or brunches. The home serves as a café, a cinema, or a hip bar. People who work in home offices also allow business partners to drop in, either via video chat or in real life. Couch-surfers even offer total strangers their couches to sleep on.

This new openness requires flexible solutions, a systematic approach and clear lines coupled with individuality and a sure instinct when selecting prominent

eye catchers. The following chapter is filled with inspirations based on this approach. Popular classics include low sideboards and armchairs plus kidney-shaped tables. These can be perfectly combined with other vintage and retro pieces, be it an antique heirloom with patina or a splash of color such as the Flowerpot by Verner Panton - the cult lamp of the 1960s is being reproduced with the old and trusted design and in many color variations.

There is also a large bandwidth of nostalgic and humorous accessories for the kitchen. Kitchenware made of enamel, the style of American diners, and resound-

ing Italian names like De'Longhi and Bialetti suggest that the host can appreciate a good espresso or prepare at a moment's notice a tasty Sunday roast in his or her Le Creuset French oven. Another icon is the rotund 1950s refrigerator. Smeg presents it in unconventional designs ranging from the Union Jack to a jeans look. Enamel-coated advertising signs are back and so is lemonade with flip-tops. The only one who is sure never to return is the efficient housewife behind the stove. This shows once again that retro does not claim that everything was better in earlier times. Instead, it is about the joy of premium design and quality.

Flowerpot

A child of his time, Panton incorporated the events of his lifetime into his designs. The Flowerpot lamp brings together the 1968 students' revolts in Paris, Rome and the US, the first moon landing in 1969, and is the epitome of Panton's theory that color could evoke feelings. The Flowerpot with its two semi-circular spheres facing each other is an icon of 1960s pop esthetic. The clean lines and bright, saturated hues, however, have endured over time, making it just as much a synonym of our time too. Whether as a pendant or a table lamp, this piece adds a splash of color to any contemporary interior, with each vibrant hue evoking a different feeling.

DESIGNERS: Verner Panton (Denmark)
MANUFACTURERS/DISTRIBUTORS: &tradition
LAUNCH: 1968 (small pendant),
1969 (desk lamp), 1971 (big pendant)

PHOTOS: &TRADITION

Mezzo Sound-board

Designed by the Stockholm-based design studio Note, Mezzo is not your typical office product. It is a sound absorber with several functions and, most importantly, its own stylistic expression. With its retro feel, it adds a touch of 'old-style elegance' and a little bit of humor to the office. Today's offices are becoming more vivid and the requirements for flexibility are increasing. Mezzo lives up to those requirements as a truly flexible sound absorber. It rolls freely in the room and also works as a whiteboard and bulletin board. Mezzo comes in two sizes and in a range of funky fabrics. This multifunctional piece of great Scandinavian design will make mind-mapping all the more fun.

DESIGNERS: Note Design Studio (Sweden)
MANUFACTURERS: Zilenzio
LAUNCH: 2012

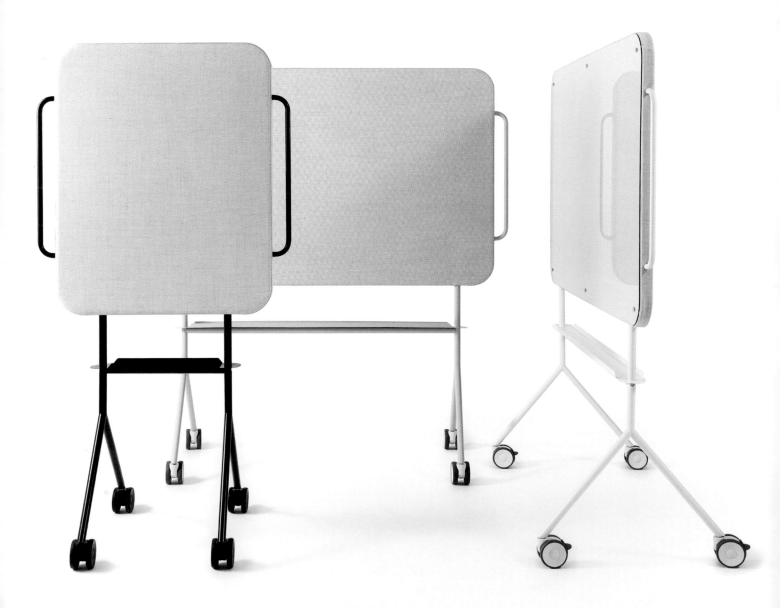

PHOTOS: MATHIAS NERO

Bialetti Moka Express

1933 saw the birth of what is still considered today one of the world's iconic Italian products: the Moka Express coffee maker. Inspired by Art Deco, it is a unique industrial design with a very simple shape, high functionality, and exceptionally long life. Slight changes were made to the shape of Alfonso Bialetti's model in the 1950s, but it remained virtually unchanged in time, with its typical aluminum octagonal shape featuring the little man with a moustache, his finger pointing upwards as the symbol of quality coffee. The Moka coffee maker led to a radical change in the habits of coffee consumption in the home and continues to be a symbol of Italian culture to this day.

DESIGNERS: Bialetti (Italy)
FOUNDER: Alfonso Bialetti
INVENTOR OF CARICATURE: Renato Bialetti
ORIGINAL: 1933
REDESIGN: 1950s/2004

HOME & DECOR

PHOTOS: BIALETTI

1382 – My First Arzberg

Arzberg's form 1382 is a cult classic that has shaped the "good form" and is exhibited as one of the few pieces of porcelain in the New York Museum of Modern Art. Designed in 1931 by industrial designer Hermann Gretsch, 1382 has been a continuous top seller for more than 80 years. In 2011 Arzberg expanded the legendary form with young customized products under the name "My First Arzberg". The collection is a successful mix of cult retro decor from the 1950s and the bold development of the legendary design icon form 1382.

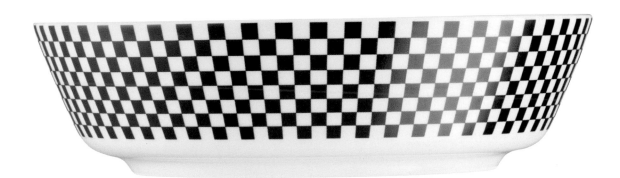

PHOTOS: ARZBERG PORZELLAN GMBH

DESIGNERS: Arzberg Porzellan GmbH (Germany)/
Heike Philipp
DESIGNER ORIGINAL: Hermann Gretsch
ORIGINAL: 1931
REDESIGN: 2011

Graphic Lamp Collection

Founded in 2008, the Portuguese lighting brand Delightfull has become internationally renowned in the past years. Its recipe for success is the skillful redesign of classic 1930s, 1940s, 1950s and 1960s models, with high-quality materials and craftsmanship. Its newest collection is an alphabet of lamps, each letter with its own style based on an iconic type font. The collection also includes numbers and symbols. Graphic collection is bold, loud, colorful, neon and very retro. The stainless steel frames add a vintage yet sleek finish to the lamps. Whether capital letters, miniscule letters, bold, italic, serif or sans-serif there's something for everyone.

DESIGNERS: Delightfull (Portugal)
MANUFACTURERS/DISTRIBUTORS: Delightfull
LAUNCH: 2013

PHOTOS: DELIGHTFULL

Upcycled Vintage Bird and Nest Teacup

Redesigned by Melody Rose, this upcycled vintage teacup and saucer with the bird and nest has been refired in the kiln at over 800 degrees, with images to re-imagine the teacup and saucer to suit modern tastes. Made from beautifully quirky upcycled vintage bone china, new life has been added to the antique and vintage pieces. The elegant jade-green color is perfectly accented with gold, making this a timeless model for any lover of fine chinaware. Small and affordable works of art, they are gorgeous displayed, but also very practical for everyday use.

DESIGNERS: Melody Rose (UK)
LAUNCH: 2011

PHOTOS: MELODY ROSE

Opinel N°8

Classic French Opinel folding knives are inexpensive, lightweight and made of superb steel. They are the standard knives of French farmers, hikers, foragers, and cyclo-tourists. In fact, almost everyone who spends time in the countryside seems to have one. They've been made since 1890 in the town of Saint-Jean-de-Maurienne in the Rhône-Alpes. The simple rotating ring that locks the blade either open or closed allows you to forgo a spring. The original handle is beech wood, a light but tough wood, making Opinel knives very light and great for use "on the road". Newer editions also include ebony, walnut, olive, bubinga, oak, or horn tip handles.

PHOTOS: OPINEL

DESIGNERS: Opinel (France/USA)
ORIGINAL: 1897
RELAUNCH: 2000

Grandy

Founded in 1867, Wesco, a German metal manufacturing company, entered the kitchenware market in 1910, producing lacquered bread and storage tins. The company has since expanded its range of products but the heritage quality has remained. In 2004 it launched Grandy, a unique retro classic bread tin reminiscent of a 1940s style. With its rounded form and characteristic metal handle it quickly reached cult status in kitchens all over the world. Its rectangular form offers a big volume, ideal for keeping bread, biscuits or cakes. The range of 15 bright and glossy finishes makes you spoilt for choice.

DESIGNERS: Wesco -
M. Westermann & Co. GmbH (Germany)
LAUNCH: 2004

PHOTOS: WESCO

Finn Juhl Sideboard

Danish designer Finn Juhl was preoccupied with shapes and colors throughout his life because of his great interest in cubist and surrealistic art. He was a pioneer of color as an active element in space, furniture and textiles. In 2013 Onecollection relaunched this piece, which is part of a theme, with cubist wood cabinets that float on delicate steel frames and wooden 'feet'. In line with Finn Juhl's fascination for Goethe's color circle, which placed colors in a harmonious cohesion, the sideboard is available in shades of yellow/red or blue combined with walnut, teak, oak, or Oregon pine.

DESIGNER ORIGINAL: Finn Juhl
MANUFACTURERS: Onecollection A/S
ORIGINAL: 1955
RELAUNCH: 2013

PHOTOS: ONECOLLECTION, ALEXIS TOUREAU (P. 73 A.)

Vintage Tins, Sweet(s) Italia

This Italian heritage brand has been producing sweet delights since 1857. The brand draws strongly on its tradition, which is the greatest source of inspiration for its quality sweets and vintage-looking packaging. The 'cult' tin boxes of these two collections have a convenient pocket size. Inspired by the Italian flag adorned with pop illustrations, they celebrate typical Italian cheerfulness, beauty, passion, creativity, and sweetness. The three vintage tins not only sport a delightful retro look in pastel colors, but even the flavors seem vintage, with the taste of spicy cinnamon and bittersweet violets.

DESIGNERS: Pastiglie Leone Marketing Dept. (Italy)
MANUFACTURERS: Pastiglie Leone
LAUNCH: 2011 (Sweet(s) Italia), 2013 (Vintage Tins)

PHOTOS: PASTIGLIE LEONE

Gazosa "La Fiorenzana"

This delicious lemonade comes from the Misox valley, which is on the southern side of the Swiss Alps. Its name was derived from an old tower in Grono in the medieval times. Right next to this tower, the Ponzio-Tonna family has been producing these fruity drinks since 1921, according to the original recipe. Several years ago the fizzy drink in bright colors and eight different flavors celebrated a comeback in the trendy bars of Zurich. The retro-style label, as well as the glass bottle with the traditional swing top, bring back nostalgic memories of hot summers and first loves. Today, the drink is still the perfect companion in the summer in the city.

PHOTOS: SARAH SBALCHIERO, ZURICH

DESIGNERS: Fabbrica Gazose (Switzerland)
MANUFACTURERS: Ponzio-Tonna family
DISTRIBUTORS: Gazosa AG
ORIGINAL: 1921
RELAUNCH: 1994

Tolix Chaise A, Fauteuil C, Tabouret H

There is no hiding the industrial heritage of the Tolix chairs — they are pure metal on metal. Xavier Pauchard created the Tolix trademark in 1927 and used it to market a range of metal furniture for use in the home, factories, offices, bars, and cafés. As a craftsman with a background in roofing, he worked hands on, developing his designs in the workshop rather than with a pencil and paper. Now recognized as classics of industrial design, his furniture pieces remain as popular as ever. The simple styling and bold colors of this stool will complement any ultra modern environment.

DESIGNERS: Xavier Pauchard (France)
MANUFACTURERS: Tolix
DISTRIBUTORS: Shop-Architect
LAUNCH: 1934-1950

PHOTOS: TOLIX

Smeg FAB28

The Italian company Smeg launched its 1950s style refrigerator FAB28 in 1997. Due to the popularity of the model, Smeg has created an entire series of esthetically coordinating appliances that nostalgically and ironically evoke the vibrant atmosphere of the 1950s. The FAB28, however, remains the star of the series, presenting itself in currently 16 different colors from soft pastel shades to bold multicolor models such as the Italian flag or the Union Jack. With curved lines, bright colors and an old-fashioned touch combined with the latest technology, this fridge has become an international interior design style icon.

DESIGNERS: Smeg SPA (Italy)
LAUNCH: 1997
REDESIGN: 2013

PHOTOS: SMEG

DESIGNERS: STANLEY - a brand of PMI (USA)
ORIGINAL: 1913
RELAUNCH: 2013

Stanley Classic Vacuum Bottle 100 Year Anniversary Limited Edition

Loved by many generations, the Stanley brand has a rich 100-year-old history. Stanley forever changed the way hot drinks are enjoyed by inventing in 1913 the all-steel vacuum flask. To celebrate the anniversary of Stanley, this iconic brand announced a Limited Edition 100 Year Anniversary Flask that pays tribute to the original vintage bottle, its history, and the stories of those who enjoy these legendary products. Part of the Stanley Classic Series, this product is built like a battleship and will keep your drink hot or cold for 24 hours.

PHOTOS: STANLEY

Cobra Table Lamp and Desk 62-Series

The Cobra floor and table lamps were the most iconic products Greta Grossman designed in the 1940s and 1950s. In 1950, the Cobra lamp won the Good Design Award and was exhibited at the Good Design Show at the Museum of Modern Art. The Cobra lamp is named for the shape of its oval shade, resembling a cobra's neck. The tubular flexible arm can be bent in all directions and the shade can be rotated 360 degree. The base is covered in powder-coated aluminum and weighted with cast iron. Although the 62-Series was designed in 1952 the pieces were deemed to be ten years ahead of their time. The slender metal legs contrast with the American walnut cube. It seems to float above the ground, giving it a sense of lightness.

DESIGNERS: Greta Grossman (Sweden)
MANUFACTURERS: Gubi
LAUNCH: 1949 (Cobra), 1952 (62-Series)

PHOTOS: GUBI

Suisse Langenthal City

In the mid 1950s, Pierre Renfer joined his father who was working as head designer for the Swiss heritage company Porzellanfabrik Langenthal. Like his father he tried to mix up the traditional conservative chinaware the company was producing with some unadorned modern, clean designs. In 1965 the City series was presented to the professional world.

Originally developed for commercial use in canteens and hospitals it was designed to require as little storage space as possible. All items are easily stackable to optimally save space. The clean and modern lines resulting from this practical aspect, however, have allowed the series to develop into a design classic of recent years.

DESIGNERS: Pierre Renfer (Switzerland)
MANUFACTURERS/DISTRIBUTORS: Porzellanfabrik
Langenthal AG
LAUNCH: 1964

PHOTOS: PORZELLANFABRIK LANGENTHAL AG

KitchenAid Artisan KSM150

2014 marks KitchenAid's 95th anniverary. Having created top quality kitchenware products ever since, the brand is synonymous with its iconic mixer that has been working in households since the 1960s. Renowned for its unparalleled mixing abilities, the model has not really changed its appearance since it was first designed. Equipped with stronger motors over the years and available in a range of bright and glossy colors, this machine is the epitome of retro design. This new model is extremely powerful and can kneed up to 1.2 kg of flour, all the while remaining extremely quiet. It features the classic tilt head and stainless steel mixing bowl that holds 4.8 1.

DESIGNERS: KitchenAid (USA)
DESIGNER ORIGINAL: Egmont Arens
DISTRIBUTORS: Novissa Haushaltgeräte AG
ORIGINAL: 1930 (model "K")
REDESIGN: 2012

PHOTOS: NOVISSA AG

Bloomingville Retro Coffee Tables

The Danish designers Bloomingville created this cute pair of 1950s style retro coffee tables, which blend nicely into any contemporary interior - be it in a cozy Nordic style or in sleek esthetics. The round triangular form combined with the grey-colored tabletop and natural bamboo legs results in a skillful mix of old and new. Through the outwardly angled legs, the tables stand firmly, whether on carpet or firm floors.

DESIGNERS: Bloomingville (Denmark)
CREATIVE DIRECTOR: Betina Stampe
MANUFACTURERS/DISTRIBUTORS: Bloomingville
LAUNCH: 2013

Plum

This set is part of the 2014 accessories collection by British designer Tom Dixon, who was honored as the "designer of the year 2014" at this year's maison & objet in Paris. This retro-looking bar set features bar and cocktail accessories made of copper or mouth-blown and hand-cut glass, taking drinking culture to a new level. The rounded forms and color combination of blue and copper give this set a very sleek and contemporary look, yet one cannot help to think of the 1960s or 1970s. This highly sophisticated set will surely be a talking point at any dinner party as you serve your dry martinis and scotch on the rocks.

DESIGNERS: Tom Dixon (UK)
LAUNCH: 2014

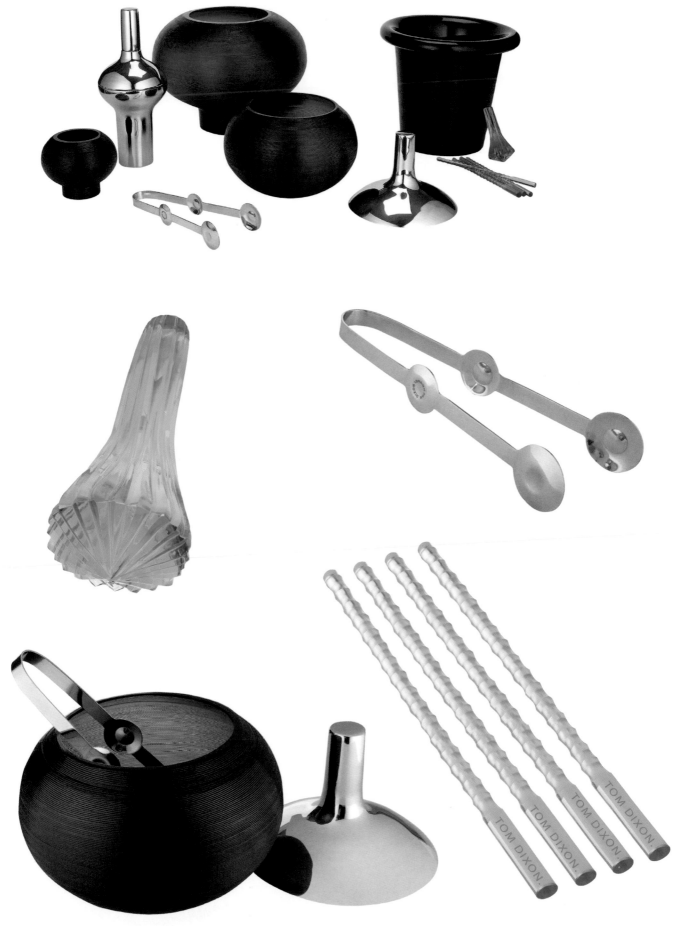

PHOTOS: TOM DIXON

AERO Stool

Inspired by canoes of the indigenous people of northern Brazil called "voadora" (literally: flying), designer Sergio Fahrer created AERO. The chair's form is reminiscent of the 1970s. However, the combination of ash wood and cream-colored leather gives the piece a very contemporary and sleek appearance. Fahrer used an exclusive method, which consists of gluing thin recycled wood layers and fabric blankets together. AERO impresses with curved, yet strict lines and could just as well be a sculpture. Put two next to each other and the effect changes completely. This piece, whether single or in pairs, lends just the right amount of retro to any contemporary interior.

DESIGNERS: Sergio Fahrer (Brazil)
MANUFACTURERS/DISTRIBUTORS: Sergio Fahrer
LAUNCH: 2002
REDESIGN: 2013

Design:
Sergio Fahrer

PHOTOS: PIERRE YVES REFALO

Ego Coffee Table

The Serbian architecture and interior design office Alter Ego Architects designed this series of multifunctional tables. They are a successful blend of retro design and minimalism, showing off their key feature right on the top panel: the patterns in bold neon colors are inspired by traditional Serbian tablecloth motifs. The combination of bright colors with traditional forms and designs make these coffee tables fun accessories for any living room. Ego Coffee Table is a prime example of the architects' design solutions, which show great attention to detail, functionality and esthetics.

PHOTOS: ALTER EGO ARCHITECTS

DESIGNERS: Alter Ego Architects (Serbia)

Form Tea Set

True to its credo, the British design studio Tom Dixon never fails to endow unique heritage pieces with a contemporary twist. This also holds true for the Form Tea Set, strongly reminiscent of the 1920s Art Deco movement with its clear geometric lines and brass material. However, there is an unmistakable modern take to this sophisticated set, which will make you want to serve British afternoon tea at any time of the day. Comprising a tea pot, jug, tea caddy (a special storage tin for loose leaf tea), milk jug, sugar dish & spoon and stamped tray, all of solid brass, the six-piece set is also highly decorative when not in use.

PHOTOS: TOM DIXON

DESIGNERS: Tom Dixon (UK)
LAUNCH: 2013

Classic Toaster, Lite Toaster

An inventor and creator, Max Gort-Barten patented his first successful product in 1946: the first flip-sided toaster. This slim yet ingenious machine formed the basis of all future Dualit designs. In the 1950s and 1960s the commercial product range experienced a steady growth, but when Dualit decided to introduce its products to the consumer market in the late 1970s, sales

veritably exploded. The toaster turned into an icon for the perfect English breakfast. Today, the heritage brand has come a long way from its first patented toaster, but nevertheless remains true to its tradition. The neat little two slot toaster boasts a glossy retro style while featuring all conveniences of a modern product.

DESIGNERS: Dualit Ltd. (UK)
INVENTOR/FOUNDER: Max Gort-Barten
ORIGINAL: 1946
REDESIGN: 1952/2013

PHOTOS: DUALIT

G Plan Vintage

In collaboration with Hemingway Design, G Plan Upholstery created G Plan Vintage, a stunning range of furniture inspired by the iconic G Plan sofas and chairs of the 1950s and 1960s. Each G Plan Vintage model is named after the year of the original model that influenced the current design. The collection embraces the quality and craftsmanship of G Plan, as well as Hemingway's fresh and vibrant approach to vintage projects. Hemingway's unique take on G Plan's retro designs resulted in a range of furniture that blends timeless details with a contemporary approach.

DESIGNERS: G Plan Upholstery Ltd. (UK)
COLLABORATING DESIGNERS: Hemingway Design
MANUFACTURERS/DISTRIBUTORS: G Plan Upholstery Ltd.
LAUNCH: 2012

PHOTOS: G PLAN VINTAGE

Anglepoise Giant 1227

Anglepoise was the ingenious result of a collaboration between automotive engineer George Carwardine and spring specialists Herbert Terry & Sons. 80 years later, Terry's archetypal Anglepoise Original 1227 lamp, based on Carwardine's pioneering perfect balance mechanism, is recognized as a British design classic. This impressive, larger-than-life, triple-scale version of the iconic Anglepoise Original 1227 injects playful, individual style into any interior space. The giant comes in a stunning range of colors, bold enough to make a statement in any interior.

DESIGNERS: Anglepoise (UK)
ORIGINAL: 1934
RELAUNCH: 2004

PHOTOS: ANGLEPOISE

Arco

The Arco lamp is one of those classic designs where form and function meet and live happily ever after. Designed in 1962 by Achille and Pier Giacomo Castiglioni, it is so practical that it seems almost obvious, but the Castiglionis' interest in ready-mades and functionalism makes this design complex in its simplicity.

The impressive chunk of Carrera marble that serves as the base is both decorative and essential to the piece's physical balance. The generous sweep of its neck makes the Arco practical and versatile, accomplishing so much with an elegant economy of form and material.

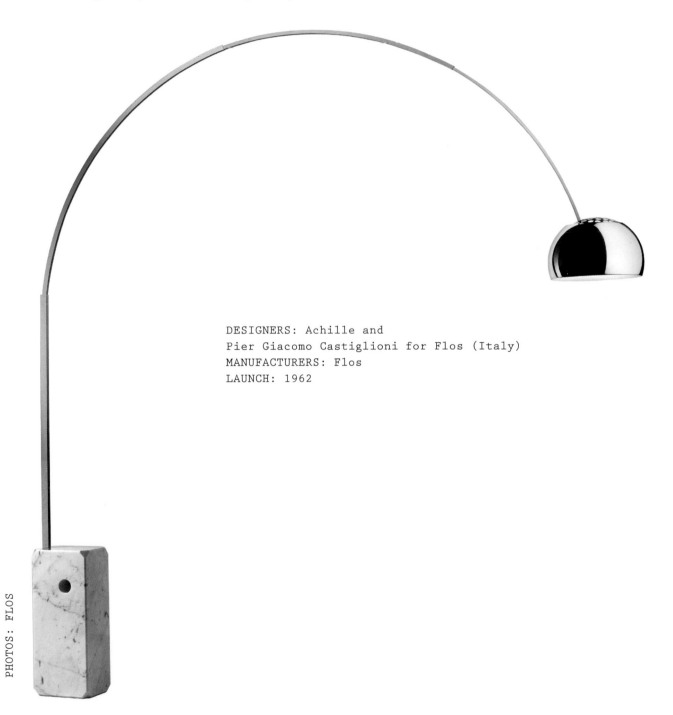

DESIGNERS: Achille and
Pier Giacomo Castiglioni for Flos (Italy)
MANUFACTURERS: Flos
LAUNCH: 1962

PHOTOS: FLOS

Bloomingville Kitchen Scale

Danish designers Bloomingville have landed a design coup with these fabulously retro kitchen scales. The scales come in two sizes (3kg or 5kg) and in a range of vintage colors, such as cream, aqua, pink, light green, yellow or orange. The silver and black versions also add a very retro stylish touch to your kitchen and make baking a pleasure. The 'crown' of the scale is a sleek steel polished dish that makes measuring and pouring as easy as it gets. An extra touch of nostalgia is added by the wide analog dial with a bright red hand.

DESIGNERS: Bloomingville (Denmark)
MANUFACTURERS/DISTRIBUTORS: Bloomingville
LAUNCH: 2013

PHOTOS: BLOOMINGVILLE

THIS

GOOD MOMS HAVE
STICKY FLOORS.
DIRTY OVENS.
AND HAPPY KIDS.

U.S. Push Can

Designed in 1920 by Sam Hammer, this iconic trash can has persisted over the decades thanks to its high quality and durability. Originally designed for the food service industry, the Push Can also entered private households with its sleek design and unmistakable push-mechanism. The original U.S. Push Can is fireproof and will extinguish flames or blazes inside it. The glossy lacquer makes the Push Can look eternally new as it is extremely robust and does not fade in the sun. Whether in private homes or in restaurants or bars, this iconic piece of design will certainly lend a retro vibe to any room.

DESIGNERS: Sam Hammer (USA)
DISTRIBUTORS: Mayer & Bosshardt AG
ORIGINAL: 1920
REDESIGN: 2014

PHOTOS: COURTESY OF THE DISTRIBUTORS

Vipp 5, Vipp 7, Vipp 9

The Vipp family business traces its beginnings to the year 1931 when Holger Nielsen starts his own metalware company. When he designed a special pedal bin for the hairdressing salon of his wife, an icon was born. Today, the business is run by one of Nielsen's daughters and her children. The brand has come a long way from the pedal bin, designing everything from faucets to kitchen modules to tableware. This set of soap dispenser, soap dish and toothbrush holder is made from high-quality stainless steel, silicone rubber and powder coating. They echo a retro feel with their round edges and bold polished brims.

DESIGNERS: Vipp (Denmark)
LAUNCH: 2005 (Vipp 9), 2009

PHOTOS: VIPP

Switches – Classique, Pierrot

In 1995 André Bousquet founded Meljac inspired by the lifestyle of the 1930s, symbolized by the drop-shaped toggle switch. His switch couples contemporary technology with the esthetics of past times. Meljac stands for quality materials, elegant shapes and refined finishes, its high-precision technology and skilled craftsmanship are combined with simple and clear lines. The sensual experience of turning on the lights obtains an entirely new meaning. While the Classique collection features a variety of brass, Pierrot presents itself in 6mm thick glass, in various colors. While the materials have their own character and qualities, they radiate a subtle vintage nostalgia in any room.

DESIGNERS: Meljac (France)
LAUNCH: 1995
REDESIGN: 2013

PHOTOS: MELJAC, M2 WWW.METRES-CARRES.FR (P. 109)

Falcon Bake Set, Prep Set, Mug

Falcon Enamelware is an iconic British homewares brand founded in the 1920s. The distinctive white and blue-rimmed pieces are considered design classics. Beautiful, yet hardwearing, they are made from porcelain enamel fused onto heavy-gauge steel, giving them durability with a smooth finish. Recently a team of young designers revitalized the brand. Since then, Falcon has been carefully redesigned with a new identity, packaging, and most of all, exciting new colors. The traditional Bake Set is now available in pillar box red or pigeon grey, it is joined by the new Prep Set, the Mug and many other drinking, baking and serving items. The new colors and extended collection give the brand a modern esthetic.

DESIGNERS: Falcon Enamelware (UK)
CREATIVE DIRECTORS: Kam and Emma Young,
Hugh Morse, Peter Hames
ORIGINALS: 1920
RELAUNCH: 2012

DESIGNERS: De'Longhi Industrial Design
Office (Italy)
MANUFACTURERS/DISTRIBUTORS: De'Longhi
COMMERCIAL LAUNCH: 2011/2012

De'Longhi Icona Vintage

Evoking the glamour, sophistication, and the excitement of 1950s Italy, De'Longhi's smart new Vintage Icona range of kettles will make a very stylish addition to any design-conscious cook's kitchen. Designed to be functional without compromising style, it's both efficient and intuitive, with great features like a water level indicator and cord-free operation for convenience. The "Icona Vintage" range features a uniquely endearing and unforgettable design that brings a touch of elegance and sophistication to any home.

PHOTOS : DE'LONGHI

Ypsilon Wallpaper

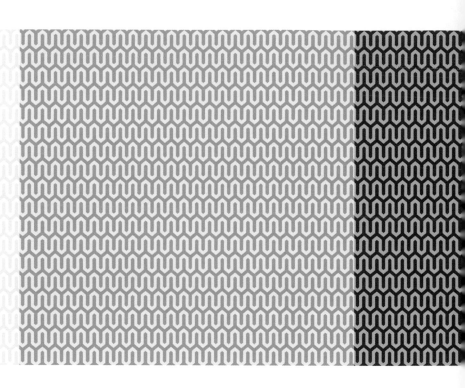

In a unique project, the Swedish
heritage brand Boråstapeter, offered
consumers wallpaper with the signature
designs of four Scandinavian designers.
Mainly known for his work in architecture and furniture design, Arne Jacobsen
also designed fabric patterns. During
World War 2 he fled to Sweden and,
while waiting to start work as an
architect again, he began to design

fabric patterns. Ypsilon follows a
clear geometry, resembling the Greek
letter, but also inspired by the static
and endless repetitions of mechanical
movements in the industrial world.
The soft colors combined with the
eternal continuity make this wallpaper
the perfect retro adornment for any
contemporary setting.

DESIGNERS: WallVision AB (Sweden)
DESIGNER ORIGINAL: Arne Jacobsen
DESIGN MANAGER: Madeleine Siderno
LAUNCH: 2012

PHOTOS: BORÅSTAPETER

SVENSKA ANTIKHANDLARE
SWEDISH ANTIQUE DEALERS

LOUIS VUITTON ARCHITECTURE

Transportation

Vintage style is as popular in fashion as it is among car lovers who collect, tend to and maintain their precious vehicles. Whether old or new, no other article of daily use evokes as many emotions as the automobile. It symbolizes freedom and independence, acts as a status symbol and a second home - ideally for decades. Its curves are sexy, its character is reliable, sporty, or noble. Last but not least, we entrust our cars with our lives every time we use them. This great emotional association turns automotive design into the supreme design discipline.

In combination with vintage designs, sophisticated engine technology incites the enthusiasm of an increasing number of car and motorcycle drivers. Classics such as the VW Beetle, the Mini Cooper and currently the Fiat 500 have repositioned themselves on the market with a fresh new look without sacrificing their unique images. While these popular compact cars have been continuously present on the streets, some legends are also being revived. In particular, retro motorcycles are up and coming, whether customized one-of-a-kind bikes constructed from original parts or high-tech models with a historical

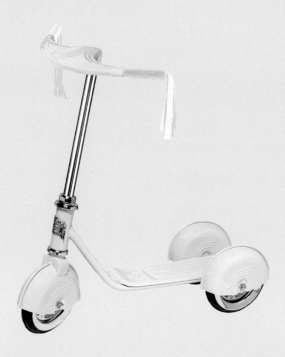

TRANSPO

exterior. Exposed engines have a special esthetic of their own. They display the engine, highlighting the direct contact to the power of the technology coupled with the charm of the original.

Bicycles are also increasing their attractive appeal. Bicycling is healthy and environmentally friendly. It not only is in line with the spirit of the time but also practical. Due to traffic congestion and lack of parking spaces in major cities, the bicycle is increasingly becoming a trusty everyday companion. Accordingly, the passion for details and styles is increasing, taking the

bicycle also back to its roots. Pedersen Bicycles is replicating historic 19th-century shapes in its sculptural frames. The Italian designer Bruno Greppi even goes further back in history. The shape of his luxurious e-bike Cykno resembles the velocipede, the ancestor of all bicycles.

These and many other examples of the following chapter tell of the joy of driving. The focus is on automotive and bicycle design. However, there are also many interesting examples of retro design in the leisure sector and in yacht design.

Caterham Seven 165

First conceived in 1957 by legendary designer Colin Chapman, the Seven was the ultimate expression of "adding lightness". Only weeks after it was designed and a few examples were built, the two-seater sports car made its debut at the Brighton Speed Trials. In 1973, Graham Nearn, founder of Caterham Cars secured manufacturing rights for the Seven. After years of building ever more powerful variants of the Seven, Caterham announced the arrival of the Seven 165 - a back-to-basics variant of the iconic sports car powered by a super-compact, turbocharged Suzuki engine. The Seven 165 is designed for lovers of the original model, who prefer vintage charm and handling finesse to performance.

DESIGNERS: Caterham Cars (UK)
DESIGNER ORIGINAL: Colin Chapman
MANUFACTURERS: Caterham Cars
ORIGINAL: 1957
RELAUNCH: 2014

PHOTOS: CATERHAM CARS LTD.

Brompton M3R

This British company won awards for its innovative folding bike, which began in the 1970s when designer Andrew Ritchie, inspired by the Bickerton folding bicycle, started designing a prototype of his own. After several prototypes, Brompton Bicycle Ltd. started production in 1981. When the Brompton won the Cyclex award for best product, its popularity increased. The Brompton always stayed true to its credo, increasing people's independence and freedom. Constantly updated, the bikes are highly reliable and durable, coveted by a large community all over the world. The newest M line Brompton is an allrounder and the most popular model. With its racing green color and brown leather saddle it sports a neat vintage look that is sure to turn heads.

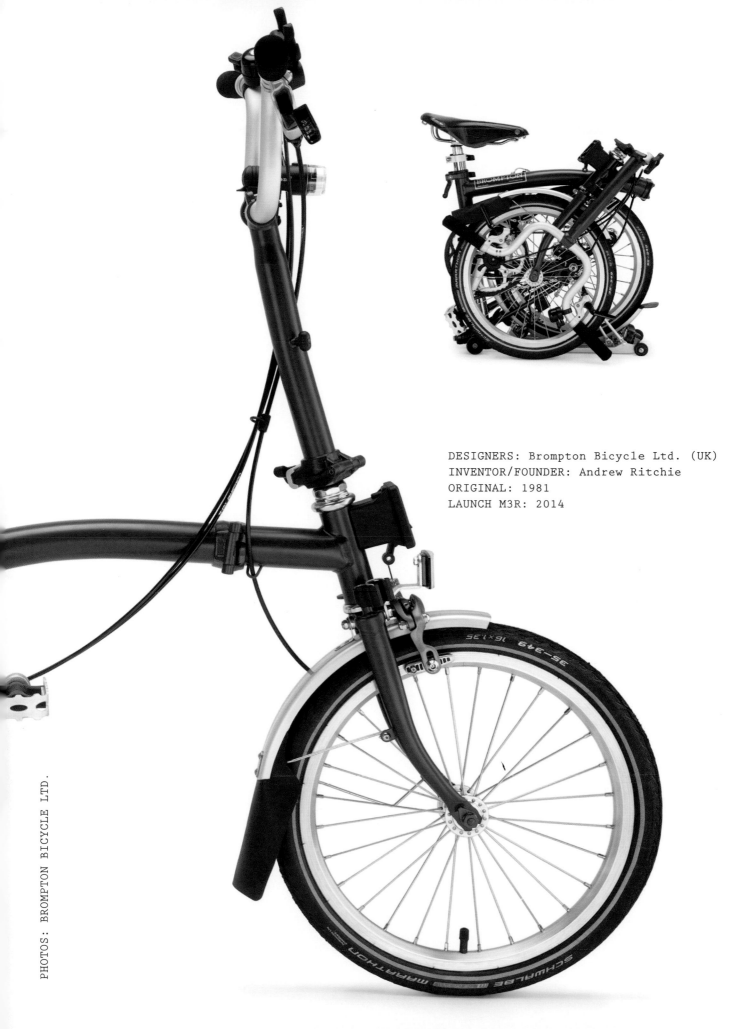

DESIGNERS: Brompton Bicycle Ltd. (UK)
INVENTOR/FOUNDER: Andrew Ritchie
ORIGINAL: 1981
LAUNCH M3R: 2014

PHOTOS: BROMPTON BICYCLE LTD.

Design:
Lars Lykkegaard

DESIGNERS: Lars Lykkegaard (Denmark)
LAUNCH: 2010

Featherbed 865

If the Featherbed 865 by Lars Lykkegaard looks like a mid-century relic, that's because it is. This vintage 1954 Norton frame exudes a retro character, but its heartbeat is decidedly modern. Under that vintage Norton gas tank is a 2010 Triumph Thruxton 865 engine, presenting a marriage of old and new representing the best of both worlds. The result is a café-style cruiser that was tested on trips down the street before embarking on a continental journey across Europe. It is a stunning achievement for Lykkegaard: a bike with a modern heart and a vintage soul.

TRANSPORTATION

PHOTOS: LARS LYKKEGAARD

Nudie Boards

These boards, designed by the British designers Nic Costa and Alby Ball, bring back the pure essence of street surfing as it was back in the 1970s. Each handmade solid wood board is crafted for the perfect ride, and will leave you wanting to get back on time and time again. The grained oak or ash is personally selected from specialist suppliers and hand shaped into the dynamic surfboard style profile. The soft transparent wheels add a bright splash of color to complete the retro-style look. Use them for long soulful turns on open roads, wide paths, or skating along seafronts, and lose yourself in the bliss of cruising the streets.

Design:
Nudie Boards

DESIGNERS: Nudie Boards (UK)
FOUNDERS: Nic Costa & Alby Ball
LAUNCH: 2013

PHOTOS: NUDIE BOARDS

Fiat 500

Retro has slowly been making a comeback in fashion, photography, and food creations. So it was no surprise when the Chrysler Group announced the unveiling of the newly modernized Fiat 500 "1957 Edition", a tribute to the original Nuova Cinquecento built in 1957. Having taken some vintage styling cues from its original ancestor, the Fiat 500 features a 16-inch retro wheel design that has a wide chromed lip, body-color accents, and a vintage FIAT logo on its center cap. The same Fiat logo can be found on the front fascia and rear lift gate. The little sportster comes in a range of bright and bold colors but also vintage pastel editions.

DESIGNERS: Fiat (Italy)
MANUFACTURERS: Chrysler Group
ORIGINAL: 1957
RELAUNCH: 2007

PHOTOS: FIAT

Kun_tiqi Orca

Combining heritage materials and techniques with eco-friendly values, Kun_tiqi produces high-quality surfboards made of Balsa wood and eco resin, which contains 55% vegetable oil. In the 1940s, surfer legend Tom Blake was the first to build hollowed out wooden surfboards. His technique became trendy and in the 1950s Balsa wood was the most popular material for manufacturing surfboards.

In addition to being incredibly light and easy to maneuver, Balsa surfboards are also durable and have a beautifully natural look. Each piece is unique and handcrafted in a production process that takes up to 40 working hours. They're worth the wait as they help to preserve the place the surfers love so much - the ocean.

DESIGNERS: Kun_tiqi (Spain)
MANUFACTURERS: Kun_tiqi
LAUNCH: 2007

PHOTOS: KUN_TIQI

Design: Kun_tiqi

Diabola V35C and Tractor V75

Product designer Stefano Venier customized any motorcycle he was driving. Turning his passionate hobby into a profession, he established Venier Customs in New York. In their Italian workshop the master mechanics redesign vintage motorcycles with customized hand-made parts. The Diabola, a cruiser from the 1980s, was stripped to the essentials and refined with a Venier custom seat pan and rear cowl. The tank has a glossy black finish with the original and weathered Moto Guzzi tank badges. The Tractor V75 is based on Moto Guzzi's polizia version of its NTX750 from the 1990s. Venier transformed it into an off-road bike with a low-key look, with the olive green finish of the tank adding a boost of style.

DESIGNERS: Venier Customs/
Stefano Venier (Italy/USA)
ORIGINALS: 1980s (Diabola), 1990s (Tractor)
REDESIGN: 2012 (Diabola), 2013 (Tractor)

PHOTOS: DONATELLO TREVISIOL

Aquariva Super by Riva

After joining one of the leading companies in luxury boats production in the world - the Ferretti Group - Mauro Micheli from Riva's design studio sat together with the Ferretti Group's naval research and design center to create the Aquariva Super, a celebration of the legendary 1960s and 1970s design classic Aquarama. With a cruising speed of 36 knots and a maximum speed of 41.5 knots, this retro beauty looks like it belongs in a James Bond movie. The soft elegant lines reflect tradition, while the beautifully carved wooden decks and leather trimmings accentuate luxury. Naturally, the boat is equipped with the latest technology to satisfy the needs of an enthusiast yearning for the good old days.

PHOTOS: FERRETTI GROUP

DESIGNERS: Officina Italiana Design (Italy)/
Mauro Micheli
MANUFACTURERS: Ferretti Group
ORIGINAL: 1962
RELAUNCH: 2010

Beach Leech

Hydroflex Skateboards produces retro skateboards inspired by the late 1970s but infused with modern technology. The decks feature a stylish honeycomb design and radiant colors. They are made of cell high density PET foam, triaxial fiberglass and high-quality epoxy resin, rendering the boards waterproof and highly durable. The Beach Leech is a retro shape mini cruiser with a perfect kicktail for tight cruising turns and pulling tricks. The unique diamond tail features a tail pocket where your foot fits right in for perfect flips and tricks.

TAHITI   REPTILE   SUNSET   YELLOW   LIME   MILITIA

PINK   ORANGE   RED   BLUE

DESIGNERS: Hydroflex Skateboards (USA)
MANUFACTURERS: Hydroflex Technology LLC
LAUNCH: 2013

PHOTOS: HYDROFLEX SKATEBOARDS

MANUFACTURERS/DISTRIBUTORS: Imperia Automobiles (Belgium)
EXTERNAL DESIGNER: Denis Stevens

Imperia GP Roadster

In an attempt to revive the Belgian heritage brand Imperia, Imperia Automobiles announced the launch of this highly innovative, yet vintage-looking roadster. The design of this highly ambitious vehicle hinges on three remarkable requirements. First: environmental concerns, implemented through the new PowerHybrid® technol-ogy, which was exclusively invented for this car. Second: the pleasure of sports driving, obtained by high-level performance. And third: a seducing neo-retro design, inspired by the Imperia history. Upon its release this car is going to be a world first in innovation and technology.

PHOTOS: ANTHONY SOETE, BELGIUM

BMW R nineT

For its 90th anniversary, BMW Motorrad has launched the R nineT. It is an unclad motorcycle inspired by the 1970s BMW R 90 S. With the R nineT BMW skillfully blends the boxer engine's rugged character and the design traits of various motorcycle eras with cutting-edge technology and a modular concept that offers a large scope of personalization. The nineT is strictly reduced to the essentials, built to cater to the many motorcycle enthusiasts who yearn for unadulterated, stress-free riding pleasure.

DESIGNERS: BMW Motorrad (Germany)
LAUNCH: 2013

PHOTOS: BMW MOTORRAD

Cykno

Vintage style design, innovative and fine materials combined with a precise made in Italy technology and production - Cykno is a work of design in movement, designed to meet the needs of low-impact mobility. Cykno is an exemplary and technically high-performance vehicle, with a refined style and an eco-friendly soul, capable of satisfying the most demanding and elegant clientele. It is difficult to consider Cykno a bicycle; Cykno is an eclectic vehicle, which was designed for conscious clients who seek sustainable mobility solutions.

DESIGNERS: Luca Scopel (Italy)
ENGINEERS: Bruno Greppi (Italy)
LAUNCH: 2013

Classic Teardrop

These retro-looking beauties are entirely handcrafted by Richard and Lyn Stark in their workshop and home in the Hertfordshire countryside. They use premium materials to create unique pieces with a lot of heart. The Teardrop is the smallest of the three models. It has room for a nice cozy double bed with some storage space and kitchen area with everything you need. The lovely color finishes in crème and light-blue add the extra vintage touch.

DESIGNERS: Richard & Lyn Stark (UK)
MANUFACTURERS/DISTRIBUTORS:
The English Caravan Company
LAUNCH: 2010

Design:
Richard & Lyn Stark

PHOTOS: RICHARD & LYN STARK

Technology & Entertainment

Retro counters high-tech. Whether smartphone, tablet or notebook, the innovation cycles are exhibiting an ever-increasing pace. Because we are constantly pressured to update, we long for deceleration. The designs of good old times promise to deliver this. At the same time, vintage and retro by no means involve foregoing the amenities of modern progress. We want both, and the ultimate combination is high-tech with a retro cover.

Actually, technological progress was the main catalyst for the popularity of all things past. Old school buddies poke us on Facebook, we bid on vintage furniture on eBay and watch Dallas on DVDs. Historical documentaries and music videos of the MTV era are only a single mouse click away on YouTube. The past has never been this accessible. There is a certain degree of irony involved when we use our smartphones to look at the good old times when telephones still had cables. The following chapter shows how creative individuals strike a balance between the opposing poles of high-technology and vintage.

The following pages present charming and unique symbioses of old and new. For example, Dominic & JP Odbert installed cutting-edge speaker technology in vintage suitcases. At the same time, the legendary Elvis microphone by Shure

TECHNOLO

is undergoing a technological update. Photography as a medium is already about remembrance, just think of the family photo album. Nevertheless, retro cameras are currently in style. Those who appreciate the feeling and handling of earlier cameras, yet do not want to forego live view and full HD video can find what they want at Leica or Hasselblad.

We may ask ourselves that if the most modern digital photography is encased in wood and leather, then what will the design of the future look like? This quickly brings to mind the key-word Apple. After all, the unadorned esthetics of the iPhone, iPod and co.

has enchanted the whole world. Yet even the minimalist computer sculptures of Jonathan Ive prove once again that progress is always related to the past. The credo of "form follows function" did not originate with the Apple chief designer. It is the philosophy of Bauhaus. If you put the iPod next to Dieter Ram's Braun pocket radio T3 of the year 1958 you will discover a stunning similarity. Technology is the future, design is tradition and only when the two come together there is room for innovation.

BoomCase

The BoomCase was born in San Francisco in 2009. Dominic Odbert was weary of constantly buying batteries for his boom box, which did not sound that great anyway. He decided to take matters into his own hands and build one of his own; after all he had the relevant knowledge. The result was the BoomCase, an original vintage suitcase equipped with a built-in rechargeable battery that will last for 14+ hours. The news about this high-tech vintage blend device spread and the rest is history. Today, each BoomCase is still hand-made in Sacramento from original vintage suitcases, and thus one of a kind.

PHOTOS: DOMINIC ODBERT, JEFF ALEXANDER (P. 149)

DESIGNERS: Dominic & JP Odbert (USA)
LAUNCH: 2010

Design:
Dominic & JP Odbert

Argus C3

Principally designed by Dr. Gustave Fassin, the Argus C3 was thrust back into the limelight by ILOTT Vintage in 2012, fully refurbished with signature real wood veneers. Inspired by the romantic ideal of pre-electronic photography, the C3 collection consists of select classic mid-century rangefinder cameras refurbished. These aren't just nice to look at, they are fully working cameras. Even with almost half a century of use and abuse behind them, with expert attention the cameras are capable of creating images as exceptional as the day they were made.

DESIGNERS: ILOTT Vintage (USA)
ORIGINAL: 1939-1966
RELAUNCH: 2012

PHOTOS: ANDREW BELLAMY/BELLAMY STUDIO. © ILOTT VINTAGE

Philco PC

SchultzeWORKS designstudio has reinvented the personal computer, called Philco PC. The design of the Philco PC was inspired by the 1954 design classic Philco Predicta, as well as an eclectic mixture of modern minimalism, the steampunk movement, and antique typewriters. As lead designer Dave Schultze explains, "the result is a design esthetic that blends multiple elements of the familiar, but with some surprisingly fresh styling that just so happens to house a state-of-the-art Windows 7 PC." The bold orange color along with the typewriter-styled keyboard make Philco PC the ultimate retro device for any office.

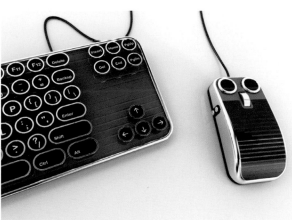

DESIGNERS: SchultzeWORKS designstudio/
Dave Schultze (USA)
LAUNCH: 2009

PHOTOS: SCHULZEWORKS DESIGNSTUDIO

Digital Bolex D16

If you don't look closely you will think this is a vintage Bolex 16mm film camera - but it is actually better. This innovative design team has combined the classic look of the Bolex hand camera with highest technology. The camera is lightweight and easy to hold with a molded pistol grip. The grip can also be removed, which allows the camera to be mounted to a rig or tripod. The D16 uses standard CF cards as storage and can be easily connected to your computer via USB. Although it is pretty cool as a retro camera for shooting home videos, the D16 also features all the options for professional use on set or in the studio.

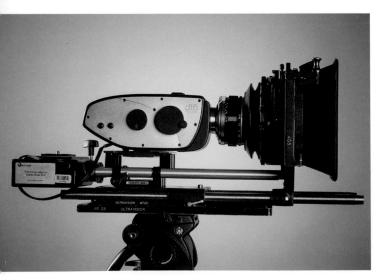

DESIGNERS: Joseph Rubinstein,
Mike Liwak, Elle Schneider (USA)
LAUNCH: 2013

PHOTOS: DIGITAL BOLEX

**Design:
Joseph Rubinstein,
Mike Liwak, Elle
Schneider**

Crosley CR 3003A Solo, CR3022 Ranchero, CR6016A Spinnerette

The Crosley CR3003A Solo has a vintage look coupled with modern technolgoy. This neat tabletop radio comes with a noble and elegant cabinet made from wood with a walnut black finish for a perfect match and integration with any home decor or furniture. Placing the speakers on the top of this little box offers a surprisingly full sound. Crosley's Ranchero might look like a vintage piece from the 1950s, but this tabletop radio in a dashing vintage look features an analog AM/FM radio tuner, but also allows connection of MP3 devices. Like in the days of Rock'n'Roll, this portable turntable allows music enjoyment everywhere. Featuring a USB connection and an outlet for MP3 players, Crosley's portable turntable is equipped with the most recent technology.

DESIGNERS: Crosley Radio (USA)
DESIGNER ORIGINALS: Powel Crosley
ORIGINALS: 1920s
RELAUNCH: 2013

PHOTOS: CROSLEY RADIO

MiniPod Bluetooth

A design icon and the model that started it all, the MiniPod is one of the world's most recognized loudspeakers. Since its launch in the early 1990s, the MiniPod had set a benchmark for what can be achieved when moving away from conventional box designs. The latest version of this groundbreaking product,

the MiniPod Bluetooth, follows the same design principles of the original model but with Bluetooth reception. The cabinet design exemplifies the term "form follows function" with each characteristic of the design having a precise acoustical justification.

DESINGERS: Simon Ghahary for Scandyna
MANUFACTURERS: Scandyna (Denmark)
LAUNCH: 1994
RELAUNCH: 2013

PHOTOS: INHOUSE FOTOGRAFI - SOEREN BAYER

iBox XC

Eclectic fans of the music players of the past are sure to adore the iBox XC by thodio, which offers impeccable design esthetics paired with modern technology to deliver a truly intriguing experience. Portable and powered by an internal rechargeable battery, the iBox XC features a 30-pin dock for connecting a MP3 device, as well as Bluetooth wireless technology to pair other products. Kevlar speakers with softdome tweeters help the iBox XC to deliver crisp highs and deep lows without the need to attach auxiliary equipment.

DESIGNERS: thodio Freedom Hifi/
Thomas Spaans (The Netherlands)
LAUNCH: 2012

Design:
thodio Freedom Hifi/
Thomas Spaans

PHOTOS: NATALY TACCOLA, THOMAS SPAANS - AMSTERDAM

TECHNOLOGY & ENTERTAINMENT 161

iTurntable and iTypewriter

At first glance these two look like a good old turntable and typewriter. At second glance, however, they turn into highly innovative designs for the iPod or iPad. The young designer Austin Yang integrates the pleasurable physical interaction of old products into contemporary technology gadgets. At the center of the turntable there is a dock for the iPod or iPhone. The arm is used to back up or skip ahead. This is like placing the needle on the vinyl - more fun than pressing a button on a touchscreen. Similarly, the iTypewriter offers the actual feeling and sound of a typewriter. These items add an authentic vintage touch to high-tech gadgets.

DESIGNERS: Austin Yang (Meng-Ju) (China/UK)
LAUNCH: 2012

Design:
Austin Yang

PHOTOS: AUS DESIGN STUDIO

Hasselblad Stellar Special Edition

Founded by Viktor Hasselblad, the Swedish heritage brand is primarily known for its production of professional cameras. The brand has collaborated with NASA and sent cameras into space. Recently, Hasselblad launched two series of cameras for the amateur and enthusiast market. The Stellar Special Edition combines Hasselblad's style with newest technology and high-quality materials. The cameras are equipped with Carl Zeiss lenses, full HD video and a 3.6x optical zoom. The wedge grip is reminiscent of a vintage design and the three premium options black with carbon, orange with wenge and white with padauk along with the luxury leather case and straps make the camera an exquisite travel accessory.

DESIGNERS: Hasselblad (Sweden)
MANUFACTURER LENSES: Carl Zeiss
LAUNCH: 2013

PHOTOS: HASSELBLAD

Crosley CR55 Wall Phone, CR59 Princess Phone, CR60 Desk Phone

These Crosley telephones are an ode to the 1950s telephone designs by Henry Dreyfuss. First and foremost his iconic desk phone, which he developed in 1949. The black phone, which quickly conquered office desks, celebrates a comeback in this vintage-looking edition by Crosley. But instead of the slow rotation of a rotary dial, the phone actually func-tions with push button technology. This is true for the other two editions as well, which Dreyfuss designed for private households. The three pieces introduce a vintage nostalgia to any home, reminding users of the good old times, when they had to stay in one place to talk on the phone.

DESIGNERS: Crosley Radio (USA)
LAUNCH: 2013

PHOTOS: CROSLEY RADIO

OTTO Ventilator

This is not your classic ventilator, it is far more stylish. Inspired by industrial ventilators in car tunnels, Martin Stadler asked designer Carlo Borer to make these black metal blades more residential-friendly. The wooden ring wrapped around the industrial fan reduced the noise and OTTO was born. This small and quirky fan will bring you the longed-for breeze on a hot summer day. Thanks to the height-adjustable feet the air circulation can easily be varied. The combination of the wooden frame, which is also available in bamboo, and the black metal give OTTO a retro appearance in line with modern design esthetics.

DESIGNERS: Stadler Form (Switzerland)
COLLABORATING DESIGNER: Carlo Borer
MANUFACTURERS: Stadler Form AG
LAUNCH: 2005

PHOTOS: STADLER FORM AG

**Design:
Stadler Form,
Carlo Borer**

Roberts Radio RD 60 Revival

Roberts Radio beautifully blends a retro leather cloth finish and wooden effect side panels with modern DAB/FM technologies. Inspired by the successful 1950s model of the brand, the RD 60 Revival features DAB+ reception, as well as normal AM/FM frequencies, a dock to plug in an external MP3 device, and a preference button to save your favorite radio station. And if you don't feel like sharing the sound, simply plug in your headphones and enjoy the RD 60 on your own and on the go – because the handy device with a carrying strap also runs on batteries. The heritage brand's testament for high quality is the Royal crest, accrediting Roberts as an official supplier to the Royal Household.

DESIGNERS: Roberts Radio (UK)
ORIGINAL: 1950s
RELAUNCH: 2012

PHOTOS: ROBERTS RADIO

BKNYdesign V-luxe

Most of us are too young to remember when televisions were black and white, and came in wooden cabinets. Nostalgics longing to transform one of today's most popular gadgets into a classic TV set will love the V-luxe iPad stand, which will make it look like an old television (with a 10" screen), especially when watching some classic black-and-white movies on it. The swivel stand allows viewing the tablet at a wide variety of angles. Each one of these stands is handmade from quality hardwoods by BKNYdesign and has a speaker cabinet built into the base for listening to tunes or the sound of movies.

Design:
Paula Anne Patterson

DESIGNERS: Paula Anne Patterson (USA)
LAUNCH: 2010

PHOTOS: HENRY DZIEKAN (EXCEPT PORTRAIT)

Shure Super 55

The Shure 55SH, also widely known as "Elvis Microphone", has been a stage icon for 70 years. Shure has improved its legendary vocal microphone with its signature satin chrome-plated die-cast casing for pure vintage look and feel. The Super 55 is suited specifically to vocal applications. A cardioid polar pickup pattern is employed to minimize sound pickup from the rear of the microphone. This allows the model Super 55 to be used in close proximity to loudspeakers without creating feedback problems, while it can perform under adverse acoustic conditions where omni-directional microphones cannot. The Super 55 guarantees a dramatically vintage performance, whether on the stage or in the studio.

DESIGNERS: Shure (USA)
MANUFACTURERS: Shure
ORIGINAL: 1939
RELAUNCH: 2013

PHOTOS: SHURE INC.

51-72T

Leica M

This German heritage brand was elemental in the history of photojournalism. Oskar Barnack invented the successful 35mm camera in 1914. The commercial launch was delayed by World War 1, but when it was presented to the public in 1925 it was a sensation. It brought photojournalism into the middle of events to allow more dynamic storytelling. Stripped down to the essentials, the Leica M combines highest technology with a design resembling the original M3 of 1954. The most versatile model in the history of Leica models, it combines functions like Live View and Full HD video capability with additional focusing methods and a new CMOS image sensor. The omission of a number suffix emphasizes the long-term significance of the systems.

DESIGNERS: Leica Camera AG (Germany)
ORIGINAL: 1954
REDESIGN: 2012

PHOTOS: LEICA CAMERA AG

TS522 Radiocubo & RR226 Radiofonografo

In 1964, auditory design was revolutionized by the release of the Radiocubo, and continued one year later with the release of the Radiofonografo, both from the Italian manufacturer Brionvega. New colors along with a unique design caused both to spread like wildfire into homes and museums across the world. The new remakes pay homage to the original designs, yet provide all the luxuries expected of a modern device: clear sound, integrated CD player, yet still as stylish as ever. Both continue to be handmade in Italy, and feature the wood and aluminum finishing we've all grown to know and love.

DESIGNERS RADIOCUBO: Marco Zanuso & Richard Sapper
DESIGNERS RADIOFONOGRAFO: Achille & Pier Giacomo Castiglioni
MANUFACTURERS: Brionvega
ORIGINALS: 1964 (Radiocubo), 1965 (Radiofonografo)
REMAKE: 2008 (Radiofonografo), 2011 (Radiocubo)

PHOTOS: BRIONVEGA

Twemco AL-30, AP-28, BQ-15, BQ-1700, QD-35

Since 1956 Twemco has been the world's only manufacturer of fully automatic flip clocks. These perpetual calendars will bring just the right flair of retro to any office, shop or home. Available in different designs, such as analog or digital, with calendar indication, or as alarm clocks they not only show you the right time, but are also a decorative element in any room. The soft clicking sound as the minutes flip by will remind you of your grandparents' pendulum clock and will soon become your favorite background noise.

DESIGNERS: Twemco (Hong Kong)
ORIGINALS: 1956

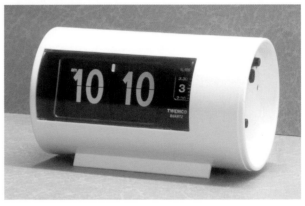

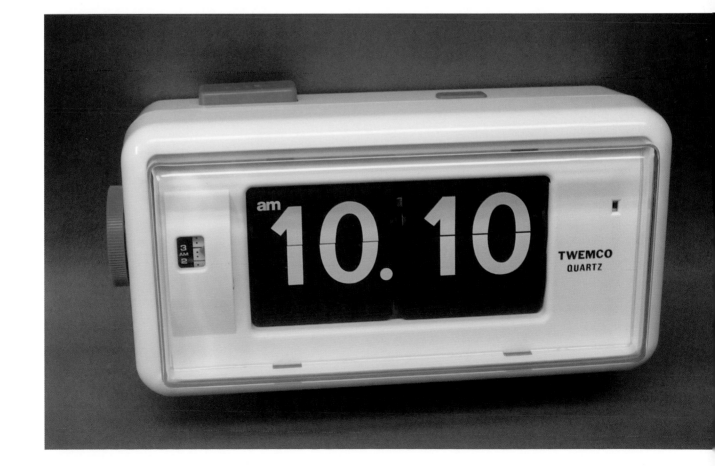

PHOTOS: TWEMCO

LOMO LC-A+

If there is one camera to be thankful for, it's the LOMO LC-A. It is the camera that started it all, the 35mm Soviet wonder that inspired a group of intrigued, creative individuals to start a movement that would later be known as the Lomographic Society International. In 2005 the LOMO factory in St. Petersburg discontinued production of the LOMO LC-A. Not about to let circumstances get in the way of creative pursuit and personal fulfillment, Lomography dared to alter the course of fate by reinventing a legend in the form of a new and improved LOMO LC-A+. The unique Minitar 1 lens delivers radiant colors, knockout contrast and shadowy vignettes that make the photos unmistakably LOMO.

DESIGNERS: Lomography (Austria)
ORIGINAL: 1984
RELAUNCH: 2006

PHOTOS: LOMOGRAPHY

Lomography x Zenit New Petzval Lens

The Lomography x Zenit New Petzval Art Lens is a stunning reinvention of the legendary Petzval lens, which was first conceived in 1840 in Vienna. A collaborative project between Lomography and Zenit, the lens is compatible with all Canon EF and Nikon F mount analog and digital cameras offering photographers and filmmakers the chance to shoot truly unique photographs and videos. Photos shot with the Petzval lens are recognizable for their sharpness and crispness in the center, strong color saturation, wonderful swirly bokeh effect, artful vignettes, and narrow depth of field. Each new Petzval lens is crafted from brass (just like the original Petzval lens) and features premium glass optics.

DESIGNERS: Lomography (Austria)
DESIGNER ORIGINAL: Joseph Petzval
MANUFACTURERS: Zenit
ORIGINAL: 1840
RELAUNCH: 2014

PHOTOS: LOMOGRAPHY

POP Phone

The POP Phone is a great way of helping to ensure enjoyment of every second of chatting on mobile phones. Available in a range of fun, bright, and funky colors, the POP Phone simply plugs into the mobile, allowing a good chat on the phone retro style. Designed by French designer David Turpin, the POP handset combines a classic style with a contemporary edge and is finished with a luxurious soft-touch texture. Fitted with a first class speaker and microphone, this handset also uses noise reduction technology for better sound quality.

DESIGNERS: David Turpin for Native Union
MANUFACTURERS: Native Union (Hong Kong)
LAUNCH: 2009

PHOTOS: NATIVE UNION

Panasonic Monitor Head-phones RP-HTX7

Vintage design meets high-end technology with these retro-style headphones. The circumaural, closed-back design keeps sound in, making them perfectly suited for public transport, travel or commuting. Soft ear cups slide along metal bands for an excellent fit and tilt adjustment. Both the ear cup cushions and the lightweight headband are wrapped in soft and elastic material with a leather look. HTX7 headphones feature a neodymium magnet with eight times more power than ordinary ferrite magnets, ensuring higher sensitivity and wide frequency response with a powerful bass, and detailed clear treble. The cool colors and retro design are an invitation to listen to Rock'n'Roll all day long.

DESIGNERS: Tsuyoshi Yoshiyama (Japan)
MANUFACTURERS/DISTRIBUTORS: Panasonic
LAUNCH: 2010

PHOTOS: PANASONIC DEUTSCHLAND GMBH

Philips Original Radio

Philips has combined retro design with modern technology to create the Original Radio - with a style to echo Philips' 1950s design classic the Philetta Radio. The radio combines an iPhone/iPad dock with 10-watt-powered speakers, DAB+ digital radio, and easy-to-use controls. The set of retro colors, such as chili red, cream, or wood finish enhance its vintage appearance. Through the clean, slightly rounded edges and silver finishing, however, the Radio adapts itself perfectly to any contemporary living space.

DESIGNERS: Philips (The Netherlands)
MANUFACTURERS/DISTRIBUTORS: Philips
ORIGINAL: 1955
RELAUNCH: 2012

PHOTOS: PHILIPS

Gramovox Bluetooth Gramophone

With Gramovox, designers Pavan Bapu and Jeff Parrish have launched the world's first Bluetooth gramophone. With its neat and elegant esthetics this device radiates a very powerful aura, and produces nostalgia. When it is not playing music, the elegantly curved neck of its steel horn along with the polished wood base make the Gramovox a piece of art and a testimony to true craftsmanship. All parts are crafted in the USA with great attention to detail. With the Gramovox, the young designers reawakened the spirit of communal bonding that gramophones promoted at the turn of the century. The Gramovox is compatible with any Bluetooth-enabled device and emits a delightfully vintage sound.

DESIGNERS: Pavan Bapu & Jeff Parrish (USA)
LAUNCH: 2013

PHOTOS: GRAMOVOX

Index

Imprint

The Deutsche Nationalbibliothek lists
this publication in the Deutsche Natio-
nalbibliografie; detailed bibliographic
data are available in the Internet at
http://dnb.dnb.de.

ISBN 978-3-03768-171-8
© 2014 by Braun Publishing AG
www.braun-publishing.ch

The work is copyright protected. Any use
outside of the close boundaries of the
copyright law, which has not been grant-
ed permission by the publisher, is un-
authorized and liable for prosecution.
This especially applies to duplications,
translations, microfilming, and any sav-
ing or processing in electronic systems.

1st edition 2014

745.2

Editorial staff:
Michelle Galindo, Sophie Steybe
Text editing:
Cosima Talhouni
Graphic concept and layout:
Michaela Prinz

All of the information in this volume has
been compiled to the best of the editor's
knowledge. It is based on the information
provided to the publisher by the designers' offices and excludes any liability.
The publisher assumes no responsibility
for its accuracy or completeness as well
as copyright discrepancies and refers to
the specified sources (designers' offices). All rights to the photographs are
property of the photographer (please re-
fer to the picture credits).